A BARTHOLOMEW MAP

WALK THE DALES

40 WALKS IN THE YORKSHIRE DALES
SELECTED & DESCRIBED BY BRIAN SPENCER

JOHN BARTHOLOMEW & SON LTD
EDINBURGH

British Library Cataloguing in Publication Data
Spencer, Brian *1931–*
    Walk the Dales.— Rev.ed.
    1. North Yorkshire. National parks: Yorkshire Dales
    National Park — Visitors' guides
    I. Title
914.28'404858
ISBN 0-7028-0800-8

Published and Printed in Scotland
by John Bartholomew & Son Ltd.,
Duncan Street, Edinburgh EH9 1TA
This revised edition published 1989.

ISBN 0-7028-0800-8

CONTENTS

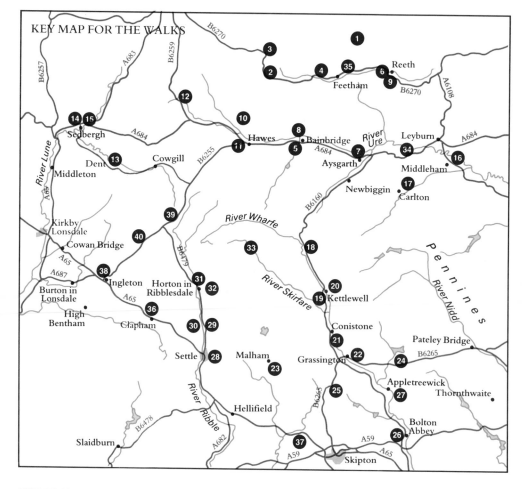

KEY MAP FOR THE WALKS

KEY TO SCALE AND MAP SYMBOLS

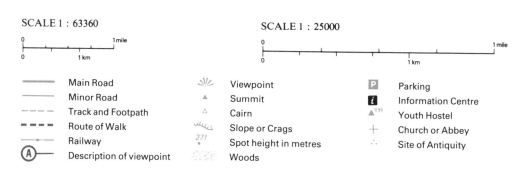

SCALE 1 : 63360

0 _____ 1 mile

0 _____ 1 km

SCALE 1 : 25000

0 _____ 1 mile

0 _____ 1 km

———————	Main Road	⚡	Viewpoint
———————	Minor Road	▲	Summit
— — — —	Track and Footpath	△	Cairn
▬ ▬ ▬ ▬	Route of Walk	⟝⟞	Slope or Crags
•————•————•	Railway	271	Spot height in metres
Ⓐ————	Description of viewpoint		Woods

Ⓟ Parking

𝒊 Information Centre

▲YH Youth Hostel

✛ Church or Abbey

∴ Site of Antiquity

1 WALKING IN THE DALES

People have walked the Yorkshire Dales almost since the first man appeared on our shores. Prehistoric hunters followed regular routes along grassy ridges and across the broad cols connecting individual dales. Later, the Romans built their roads, some of which are now used by modern traffic. Others are still recognisable as stony tracks across the fells. One of them, across Cam Fell, appears in this guide. Drovers and pack-horsemen, the ancestors of today's long-distance lorry drivers, created green roads which can be traced for miles across the wild central moors. Corpse roads linking outlying hamlets to sanc-tified ground miles down the dale still exist but it is perhaps the local footpaths, connecting villages and farmsteads, which will give the most pleasure to a walker in the Dales.

Walking is a sport which can fulfil the needs of everyone. You can adapt it to suit your own preferences and it is one of the healthiest of activities. Your inclination might be to walk two or three miles along a gentle track instead of one of the more arduous long-distance routes but, whatever the walk, it will always improve your general well-being. Walking should be anything from an individual pastime to a family stroll, or maybe a group of friends enjoying the fresh air and open spaces of our countryside. There is no need for walking to be competitive and, to get the most from a walk, it shouldn't be regarded simply as a means of covering a given distance in the shortest possible time.

As with all other outdoor activities, walking is safe provided a few simple commonsense rules are followed:

a) Make sure you are fit enough to complete the walk.

b) Always try to let others know where you intend going.

c) Be clothed adequately for the weather and always wear suitable footwear.

d) Always allow plenty of time for the walk, especially if it is longer or harder than you have done before.

e) Whatever the distance you plan to walk, always allow plenty of daylight hours unless you are absolutely certain of the route.

f) If mist or bad weather come on unexpectedly, do not panic and try to remember the last certain feature which you have passed (road, farm, wood, etc.). Then work out your route from that point on the map but be sure of your route before continuing.

g) Do not dislodge stones on the high edges: there may be climbers or other walkers on the lower crags and slopes.

h) Unfortunately, accidents can happen even on the easiest of walks. If this should be the case and you need the help of others, make sure that the injured person is safe in a place where no further injury is likely to occur. For example, the injured person should not be left on a steep hillside or in danger from falling rocks. If you cannot leave anyone with the injured person, and even if they are conscious, try to leave a written note explain-ing their injuries and whatever you have done in the way of first-aid treatment. Make sure you know exactly where you left them and then go to find assistance. If you meet a National Park Ranger, tell him or her what has happened. Otherwise, make your way to a telephone, dial 999 and ask for help. Unless the accident has happened within easy access of a road, it is the responsibility of the police to arrange evacua-tion. Always give accurate directions on how to find the casualty and, if possible, give an indica-tion of the injuries involved.

i) When walking in open country, learn to keep an eye on the immediate foreground while you admire the scenery or plan the route ahead. This may sound difficult, especially to a beginner but, once you can adapt to this method, your enjoy-ment will increase.

j) It's best to walk at a steady pace, always on the flat of the feet as this is less tiring. Try not to walk directly up or downhill. A zig-zag route is a more comfortable way of negotiating a slope. Running directly downhill is a major cause of erosion on popular hillsides.

k) When walking along a country road, walk on the right, facing the traffic. The exception to this rule is, when approaching a blind bend, the walker should cross over to the left and so have a clear view and also be seen in both directions.

l) Finally, always park your car where it will not cause inconvenience to other road users or prevent a farmer from gaining access to his fields. Make sure that you lock your car and hide any valuables before leaving or, preferably, carry them with you.

2 EQUIPMENT

Equipment, including clothing, footwear and rucksacks, is essentially a personal thing and depends on several factors, such as the type of activity planned, the time of year and weather likely to be encountered.

All too often, a novice walker will spend pounds on a fashionable jacket but will skimp when it comes to buying footwear or a comfortable rucksack. Blistered and tired feet quickly remove all enjoyment from even the most exciting walk and a poorly balanced rucksack will soon feel as though it is carrying half a hundredweight. Well designed equipment is not only more comfortable but, being better made, it is longer lasting.

Clothing should be adequate for the day. In summer, remember to protect your head and neck, which are particularly vulnerable in a strong sun. Wear light woollen socks and lightweight boots or strong shoes. A spare pullover and waterproofs carried in the rucksack should, however, always be there in case you need them.

Winter wear is a much more serious affair. Remember that once the body starts to lose heat, it becomes much less efficient. Jeans are particularly unsuitable for winter wear and can sometimes even be downright dangerous.

Waterproof clothing is an area where it pays to buy the best you can afford. Make sure that the jacket is loose-fitting, windproof, has a generous hood and comes down at least to knee level. Waterproof overtrousers will not only offer complete protection in the rain but they are also windproof. Do not be misled by flimsy nylon 'showerproof' affairs. Remember, too, that garments made from rubberised or plastic material are heavy to carry and wear and they trap body condensation. Your rucksack should have wide, padded carrying straps for comfort.

It is important to wear boots that fit well or shoes with a good moulded sole – blisters can ruin any walk! Woollen socks are much more comfortable than any other fibre. Your clothes should be comfortable and not likely to catch on twigs and bushes. In winter, it's best to take two lightweight jumpers, one at least with a crew neck. You will find this better than wearing one jumper made of heavy material. A woollen hat, which can be pulled well down, is essential in winter.

A piece of semi-rigid plastic foam carried in the rucksack makes a handy and yet almost weightless seat for open-air picnics.

An area map, as well as this guide, is useful for accurate navigation and it adds to the enjoyment of a walk. Finally, a small first aid kit is an invaluable help in coping with cuts and other small injuries.

3 PUBLIC RIGHTS OF WAY

Although most of the area covered by this guide comes within the authority of the Yorkshire Dales National Park, this does not mean that there is complete freedom of access to walk anywhere. Most of the land within the park is privately owned and what might appear to be an ideal spot for a picnic, or somewhere to exercise the dog, is often part of another person's livelihood.

In 1949, the National Parks and Access to the Countryside Act tidied up the law covering rights of way. Following public consultation, maps were drawn up by the Countryside Authorities of England and Wales to show all the rights of way. Copies of these maps are available for public inspection and are invaluable when trying to resolve doubts over little-used footpaths. Once on the map, the right of way is irrefutable.

Right of way means that anyone may walk freely on a defined footpath or ride a horse or pedal cycle along a public bridleway. No-one may interfere with this right and the walker is within his rights if he removes any obstruction along the route, provided that he has not set out purposely with the intention of removing that obstruction. All obstructions should be reported to the local Highways Authority.

Free access to footpaths and bridleways does

mean that certain guidelines should be followed as a courtesy to those who live and work in the area. For example, you should only sit down to picnic where it does not interfere with other walkers or the landowner. All gates must be kept closed to prevent stock from straying and dogs must be kept under close control — usually this is interpreted as meaning that they should be kept on a leash. Motor vehicles must not be driven along a public footpath or bridleway without the landowner's consent.

A farmer can put a docile mature beef bull with a herd of cows or heifers, in a field crossed by a public footpath. Beef bulls such as Herefords (usually brown/red colour) are unlikely to be upset by passers-by but dairy bulls, like the black and white Friesian, can be dangerous by nature. It is, therefore, illegal for a farmer to let a dairy bull roam loose in a field open to public access.

Most public rights of way within the Yorkshire Dales National Park have been clearly defined and are marked as such on available maps. They are marked on the Ordnance Survey one inch (1:63360) and metric (1:50000) maps as red dots for footpaths and red dashes for bridleways. On the OS 1:25000 scale, the dots and dashes are green (red dots and dashes on the 1:25000 Outdoor Leisure Maps indicate concessionary footpaths and bridleways respectively). All of the walks in this guide cover routes which follow the public right of way, or concessionary footpaths.

4 THE COUNTRY CODE

The Country Code has been designed not as a set of hard and fast rules, although they do have the backing of the law, but as a statement of common-sense. The code is a gentle reminder of how to behave in the countryside. Walkers should walk with the intention of leaving the place exactly as it was before they arrived. There is a saying that a good walker 'leaves only footprints and takes only photographs', which really sums up the code perfectly.

Never walk more than two abreast on a footpath as you will erode more ground by causing an unnatural widening of paths. Also try to avoid the spread of trodden ground around a boggy area. Mud soon cleans off boots but plant life is slow to grow back once it has been worn away.

Have respect for everything in the countryside, be it those beautiful flowers found along the way or a farmer's gate which is difficult to close.

Stone walls were built at a time when labour costs were a fraction of those today and the special skills required to build or repair them have almost disappeared. Never climb over or onto stone walls; always use stiles and gates.

Dogs which chase sheep can cause them to lose their lambs and a farmer is within his rights if he shoots a dog which he believes is worrying his stock.

The moors and woodlands are often tinder dry in summer, so take care not to start a fire. A fire caused by something as simple as a discarded cigarette can burn for weeks, once it gets deep down into the underlying peat.

When walking across fields or enclosed land, make sure that you read the map carefully and avoid trespassing. As a rule, the line of a footpath or right of way, even when it is not clearly defined on the ground, can usually be followed by lining up stiles or gates.

5 MAP READING

Some people find map reading so easy that they can open a map and immediately relate it to the area of countryside in which they are standing. To others, a map is as unintelligible as ancient Greek! A map is an accurate but flat picture of the three-dimensional features of the countryside. Features such as roads, streams, woodland and buildings are relatively easy to identify, either from their shape or position. Heights, on the other hand, can be difficult to interpret from the single dimension of a map. The one inch (1:63360) maps indicate every 50 foot contour line, while the metricated 1:25000 and 1:50000 maps give the contours at 10 metre intervals. Summits and spot heights are also shown.

The best way to estimate the angle of a slope, as shown on any map, is to remember that if the contour lines come close together then the slope is steep — the closer the steeper.

Learn the symbols for features shown on the map and, when starting out on a walk, line up the map with one or more feature, which is recognisable both from the map and on the ground. In this way, the map will be correctly positioned relative to the terrain. It should only be necessary to look from the map towards the footpath or objective of your walk and then make for it! This process is also useful for determining your position at any time during the walk.

Let's take the skill of map reading one stage further: sometimes there are no easily recognisable features nearby: there may be the odd clump of trees and a building or two but none of them can be related exactly to the map. This is a frequent occurence but there is a simple answer to the problem and this is where the use of a compass comes in. Simply place the map on the ground, or other flat surface, with the compass held gently above the map. Turn the map until the edge is parallel to the line of the compass needle, which should point to the top of the map. Lay the compass on the map and adjust the position of both, making sure that the compass needle still points to the top of the map and is parallel to the edge. By this method, the map is orientated in a north-south alignment. To find your position on the map, look out for prominent features and draw imaginary lines from them down on to the map. Your position is where these lines cross. This method of map reading takes a little practice before you can become proficient but it is worth the effort.

It is all too easy for members of a walking group to leave map reading to the skilled member or members of the party. No one is perfect and even the best map reader can make mistakes. Other members of the group should take the trouble to follow the route on the map, so that any errors are spotted before they cause problems.

Once you become proficient at map reading, you will learn to estimate the length of time required for a walk. Generally, you should estimate an extra 5 minutes for every 100 feet (30.5m) you walk uphill.

6   THE YORKSHIRE DALES NATIONAL PARK

In many other countries, National Parks are wilderness areas, where few people live unless they are connected with running the park. Countries such as the United States of America have even gone to the length of moving residents off land designated as a National Park. In England and Wales, National Parks are areas of outstanding beauty where people still live and work. One of the major functions of a National Park is to preserve the landscape and the livelihoods of the people living within its boundaries. This is achieved by careful planning control. The National Parks and Access to the Countryside Act of 1949 led to the formation of the nine National Parks in England and Wales.

The word 'National' in the title sometimes leads to misunderstanding. National Parks are not nationalised or in any way owned by the government.

The Yorkshire Dales National Park was formed in 1953 and covers an area of approximately 680 square miles (1760 sq.km). It is controlled by a committee nominated by the North Yorkshire County Council and representatives of three district councils, whose areas encroach into the park: Craven, Richmondshire and South Lakeland. This committee is augmented by a further eight members (one third of the total) appointed by the Secretary of State for the Environment to represent the wider national interests in this national asset.

Large areas of grouse moorland, mainly in the south of the park are held by the Chatsworth Estates Trust for the Duke of Devonshire. Rights of Way cross several of the moors but, most importantly, the estate allows free access to Barden and Simonseat Moors above Bolton Abbey on either side of Wharfedale. This means that walkers have the right to roam freely over the moors on all but publicised days during the shooting season or during periods of high fire risk. This concession is one which must be respected by all users.

One of the statutory functions of a Park Authority is the appointment of full-time and voluntary Park Rangers. These are people with particular knowledge of some aspects of the local environment who are available to give help and advice to visitors.

There are six full-time Information Centres based at: Aysgarth, Clapham, Grassington, Hawes, Malham and Sedbergh, together with Tourist Information Centres at Bentham, Brough, Harrogate, Ilkley, Ingleton, Kirkby Lonsdale, Kirkby Stephen, Knaresborough, Leyburn, Pateley Bridge, Richmond, Ripon and Settle on the outskirts of the park. A number of village shops throughout the Dales can now give local information on holiday accommodation, sell walking guides and offer other information to back up the full-time Information Centres. These shops are at: Askrigg, Bolton Abbey, Buckden, Dent, Gunnerside, Hebden, Horsehouse, Horton, Kettlewell, Langcliffe, Litton, Muker, Reeth and Stump Cross.

There is an Outdoor Study and Recreation Centre at Whernside Manor in Dentdale, where residential and day courses are offered by the National Park Authority in subjects ranging from fell walking to caving and general field studies. Cycle tours are organised and special rambling weekends are arranged throughout the year.

7 WHAT ARE THE YORKSHIRE DALES?

The Central Pennines are cut by a series of valleys which have become known as the Yorkshire Dales. Radiating from a watershed on the mass of high ground north and east of Ribblehead, five rivers, the Swale, Ure, Nidd, Wharfe and Aire, eventually flow east into the North Sea by way of the Ouse and Humber. Three others, the Ribble, Lune and Eden, all enter the Irish Sea, to the west, as independent rivers. All have their birth on the gritstone cap of the central moors but, with the exception of the Nidd and Lune, they all flow for at least their middle sections through countryside based upon limestone. As a result, the rivers have carved deep clefts through the soluble limestone rock to reach harder, watertight shales and slates.

Every dale has its own character. In the north, Swaledale is the wildest, a deep-cut gorge below rolling heather moors, joined by its even wilder tributary, Arkengarthdale, at Reeth where the dale begins to take on a gentler aspect. Villages of stone-built cottages line its northern banks. Place names can be traced to the early Viking settlers.

The next east-flowing dale is Wensleydale, the only one which does not take its name from its river, in this case the Ure. Wensleydale was once filled by a glacial lake and its flatter valley bottom and wider aspect is the result. Lush meadowlands feed the dairy cattle which produce milk for the famous Wensleydale cheese. The dale is renowned for its waterfalls but less appreciated features are in its four side dales, all roughly parallel to each other, which flow from the south-west. These

often secluded valleys will reward anyone who wants to explore their secrets.

Next is Nidderdale, a little-known dale to the east of Wharfedale, where the strangely-worn shapes of Brimham Rocks cut into the skyline. In fact, Nidderdale is not part of the Yorkshire Dales National Park.

Wharfedale and Airdale, with their ease of access from the West Riding, are probably the best known dales. Wharfedale, wooded in its lower reaches, is lined with dramatic limestone formations and attractive villages, a feature echoed by its tributary, Littondale, for all except its sombre headwaters. Airedale's Malham Cove, an amphitheatre of solid limestone, is an outstanding feature of the Dales. A tributary of the Aire flows from its base – the main river still flows underground at this point. The ravine of Gordale Scar, a 'roofless' cave, is close by.

Of the western dales, Ribblesdale is essentially a limestone dale separating the three highest summits of the Dales, Whernside, Ingleborough and Penyghent. Like the other northern rivers which flow into the Irish Sea, its waters are clean enough to welcome sea trout and salmon. It is the Lune's tributaries, Dentdale and Garsdale which are completely within the boundaries of the National Park, the main dale mostly skirting the north-west edge. Of the Eden, only its highest tributary, Hell Gill with its fantastic ravine, is within the park, its headwaters forming the county boundary of Cumbria and North Yorkshire, a boundary followed by the National Park.

The earliest settlers in the Dales were the hunters who lived in caves such as Victoria Cave above Settle, where the remains of reindeer and bones of grizzly bears have been found, animals which lived on the tundra-like conditions following the Ice Age. As man became more settled he built enigmatic cairns and stone circles, the use of which we can only surmise. With the Roman invasion, roads began to appear across the fells and forts were built to control lead mining areas. Lead increased in value with the expansion of building from Roman times, through the height of monastic power right up to the 19th century when cheaper imports killed off the local industry with devastating effect. Remains of the old lead mines and their smelt houses can still be found on the moors above Swaledale and Wensleydale in the north and near Grassington in the south.

Monasteries developed in the Middle Ages to cement an enforced peace made after the Norman Conquest. With their power, which only ended with the Dissolution in the 16th century, they exploited the riches of the lead mines and encouraged the development of vast flocks of sheep which roamed unhindered for miles across the fells, setting the scene for farming patterns which have changed only in recent years. The next development to take place was the movement of animals and goods across the moors; animals were driven south from Scotland and the Dales by a tough breed of men known as drovers. These men slowly moved their charges to the rapidly growing industrial areas further south, by routes which can still be traced to this day. Many of the old drove roads and pack-horse routes are still clearly defined as 'green roads', which snake for miles across the high fells and limestone plateaux of the Dales.

Today's Dalesman retains much of the character of his forebears, generally taciturn, but once you have broken through his natural reserve he becomes a friend and informant of the background to the fascinating life and environment of the Dales. The Dales themselves have a character all of their own, unique within the British Isles; like their people, the Dales need to be understood to be appreciated.

8 GEOLOGY

Almost 300 million years ago, the rocks which, today, are the lowest part of the Yorkshire Dales, existed as the muddy floor of a shallow tropical sea. Those muds became slates, the bedrock of many of the Dales' rivers. Gradually the sea filled with the teeming life of tiny crustaceans living amongst long-stemmed waterlily-like plants. As these plants and animals died, their bodies and shells sank slowly to the bottom of the sea, consolidating to form the collosal limestone cover which features so predominantly throughout the Dales. Much later, a huge river delta began to fill this sea, its outer deposits spreading to form shales, and on top of them came the harder gritstones, now the top-most rocks of the highest peaks.

As all this building up and smothering was taking place, land masses moved and gradually the land which was once in the tropics moved north towards its present position. During all this activity, faults occurred in the surface of the land. Rocks moved up and down; Malham Cove is a good surface example of a fault line.

While the land was beginning to settle into its present shape, subterranean activity forced hot mineral solutions of ores into narrow cracks in the upper rocks. These mineral solutions were mostly lead but there were traces of silver and even gold. Chemical reactions formed calcium fluoride, which was a nuisance to later miners but is a useful raw material today. To the north, vast upsurges of basalt created the columns of the Whin Sill.

Around 10,000 years BC, the land, though covered by ice, was beginning to take on the outline of the Dales as we know them. As the ice melted, moraine dams created lakes in areas such as Upper Wensleydale. Mud made from ground down rocks of the high tops began to form the basis of new strata and the process of wearing down and building up began again. In geological time 10,000 years is like a few minutes to us and, once the moraine dams were breached, those muds and clays began to form the basis of today's rich pastures of the Central Dales. The process is continuing.

9 WILDLIFE IN THE DALES

Wildlife habitats follow closely-defined zonal limits; on the high tops of Ingleborough and Penyghent, habitats are restricted to mosses and a little grass with alpine flowers, such as purple saxifrage (*Sax oppositifolia*), living in tiny crevices and ledges on the limestone crags. Mountains with broader summits, such as Whernside, are able to support coarse grasses, with heather and bilberry dominating the grouse moors further south. Meadow pipits and ring ouzels frequent the higher slopes and the dipper follows streams high on the fell. Birds of prey such as kestrels, merlins and buzzards, as well as the ubiquitous crow, can be found on most of the quieter fells. Mountain hares are often seen gambolling on the open hillsides. Even though standing water is rare on the normally dry cols and ridges, sea-birds, such as black-headed gulls, nest far from their 'official' home. For centuries, the land below the 1700 foot (520m) contour, has been improved for sheep grazing and true native grasses and rushes will only be found in areas of poor husbandry and under-grazing. Mountain pansy (*viola lutea*), rock rose (*helianthemum chamaecistus*) and thyme (*thymus serpyllum*), grow on sparse limestone soils. Limestone pavements are cracked and fissured by 'grikes' where the shade-loving plants such as dog's mercury (*mercuriatis perennis*) and hart's tongue fern (*phyllitis scolopendi*) are the remains of ground cover of native ash woods which covered the Dales before the last Ice Age.

Where the river-banks are uncultivated, natural woodland takes advantage of the rich damp soil and woodland flowers grow in profusion. Many of the rivers have excellent fish stocks but the best by far are the Lune and Ribble and their tributaries. Both main rivers manage to enter the Irish Sea relatively unpolluted and, as a result, are visited by migrant trout and spawning salmon.

10   LONG-DISTANCE WALKS

Pennine Way: the first long-distance walking route in Britain. Starts from Edale in Derbyshire and follows a high-level route to Kirk Yetholm in the Scottish Borders. Enters the Yorkshire Dales at Gargrave and takes a more or less northerly course to Tan Hill and beyond.
Dales Way: from Ilkley, the way follows Wharfedale, then by way of Dentdale to Bowness-on-Windermere in the Lake District.
Coast to Coast: across the North of England from St. Bees Head on the Cumbrian Coast to Ravenscar on the North Yorkshire coast.
Ribble Valley Way: follows the river Ribble from its source to the sea near Preston in Lancashire.

11   SHOW CAVES OPEN TO THE PUBLIC

Ingleborough Cave: at the head of Clapdale. It can only be approached by footpath from Clapham or on the return from walks on Ingleborough.
Stump Cross Caverns: on the B6265 between Pateley Bridge and Grassington. A moorland footpath links the cave with Grimwith Reservoir.
White Scar Cave: at the side of the B6255 north-east of Ingleton. Could be visited as an extension to the Ingleton's Waterfalls walk.

12   USEFUL ADDRESSES

Yorkshire Dales National Park
Hebden Road
Grassington
Nr Skipton
Yorkshire BD23 5LB (Tel: Grassington 752748)

Yorkshire Wildlife Trust Ltd
20 Castlegate
York YO1 1RP (Tel: York 59570)

National Park Information Centres:
Aysgarth Falls (Tel: Aysgarth 424); Clapham (Tel: Clapham 419); Grassington (Tel: Grassington 752748); Hawes (Tel: Hawes 450); Malham (Tel: Airton 363); Sedbergh (Tel: Sedbergh 20125).
Dales-Rail (Settle–Carlisle line and bus links):
C/o Yorkshire Dales National Park (see address and telephone number above).
Yorkshire Dales Railway (short length of track with a good collection of steam locomotives which are run at weekends and bank holidays in summer): Embsay, Nr Skipton (Tel: Skipton 4727).

13   LOW-PRICED HOLIDAY ACCOMMODATION

DALES BARNS:
Barden Tower (Tel: Burnsall 630); Catholes Farm (Tel: Sedbergh 20334); Dub Cote Farm (Tel: Horton in Ribblesdale 238); Grange Farm (Tel: Kettlewell 259); Skirfare Bridge (Tel: Grassington 752465); Hill Top Farm (Tel: Airton 320).

YOUTH HOSTELS
Malham (Tel: Airton 321); Stainforth (Tel: Settle 3577); Linton (Tel: Grassington 752400); Dent (Tel: Dent 251); Ingleton (Tel: Ingleton 41444); Aysgarth (Tel: Aysgarth 260); Kirkby Stephen (Tel: Kirkby Stephen 71793); Grinton Lodge (Tel: Richmond 84206); Hawes (Tel: Hawes 368); Keld (Tel: Richmond 86259); Kettlewell (Tel: Kettlewell 232).
Further details from:
YHA Yorkshire Area Office
96 Main Street
Bingley BD16 2JH
West Yorkshire (Tel: Bradford 567697)

Walk 1
BOOZE
3¼ miles (5.2 km) Easy

```
0                                                    1 mile
|----------|----------|----------|----------|----------|
0                              1 km
```

Followers of the popular TV series, *All Creatures Great and Small*, will instantly recognise the bridge in Langthwaite, where this walk starts, as the one used in the opening shots of each episode. The walk explores part of Arkengarthdale from the village of Langthwaite, a little under 4 miles (6.4 km) north of Reeth along the Tan Hill road. Limited parking can usually be found on the main road near the start of the walk.

3 *At the top of the rocky field, go through a gate and follow a track to the right, across the heather moor.*

4 *On reaching the boundary wall, follow it to the left as far as a barn. Climb a stile on the right and follow the sunken field path downhill.*

2 *Climb to open fields above woodland and go past a ruined farmhouse. Turn right through a wicket gate marked by a finger post. There is no path so bear slightly right, uphill.*

5 *Turn left along the lane into the farm hamlet of Booze.*

6 *Turn right through the stockyard at Town Farm. There is no path but go down the middle of two adjacent fields towards the valley bottom.*

Arkengarthdale

Booze Common

Arkle Beck

(B)

(A)

Langthwaite

(C) Booze

Slei Gill

(D)

Strothwaite Hall

1 *Take the side turning away from the main road and go over the hump-backed bridge. Cross the square with the Red Lion Inn to one side and fork left on an upward-slanting woodland path.*

8 *Do not cross the footbridge on your left but continue upstream along the riverside track into Langthwaite.*

7 *Bear right along a grassy path above the stream, then right again into the main valley.*

A Viewpoint. Langthwaite was the centre of lead mining activity in Arkengarthdale until about 1890, when cheap imports killed off the industry and the valley became de-populated. Scars left by 'hushing', a system where deliberate flooding of part of the hillside revealed the underlying ore-bearing strata, can still be seen on the fells, together with spoil heaps near crushing plant or mine entrances. The most famous mine is the C.B. on the opposite hillside, named after its 18th-century founder Charles Bathurst. **Always take care near the ruined buildings and never try to enter any of the mine workings.**

B Viewpoint. Arkengarthdale is below with Swaledale beyond and to your left.

C Booze. Unfortunately, having no pub, the name of this tiny hamlet has nothing to do with alcoholic refreshment but it possibly refers to 'bouse', a mining term for undressed lead ore. Narrow and rocky Slei Gill is to the left, a valley which still bears the scars of lead mining.

D The path goes through a pretty riverside wood, which is filled with bluebells each spring.

12

Walk 2
MUKER AND THWAITE
3 miles (4.8 km) Easy

Both of the villages visited on this walk were founded by Norse settlers. Starting in Thwaite near the junction of the Buttertubs Pass road with the B6270 (before the latter climbs into the upper reaches of Swaledale), the route climbs the southern slope of Kisdon Hill with its glorious views of the dale. From Muker (pronounced 'Mooker'), a field path leads back to Thwaite. You can park in the centre of Thwaite although spaces are limited. It is possible to join Walk 3 (Kisdon Hill) at pointer no.3 of this walk to make a longer whole-day route.

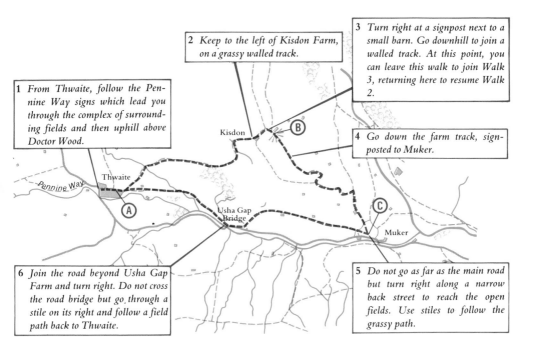

2 *Keep to the left of Kisdon Farm, on a grassy walled track.*

3 *Turn right at a signpost next to a small barn. Go downhill to join a walled track. At this point, you can leave this walk to join Walk 3, returning here to resume Walk 2.*

1 *From Thwaite, follow the Pennine Way signs which lead you through the complex of surrounding fields and then uphill above Doctor Wood.*

4 *Go down the farm track, signposted to Muker.*

5 *Do not go as far as the main road but turn right along a narrow back street to reach the open fields. Use stiles to follow the grassy path.*

6 *Join the road beyond Usha Gap Farm and turn right. Do not cross the road bridge but go through a stile on its right and follow a field path back to Thwaite.*

A Thwaite. The name is Old Norse for a woodland clearing, an indication of the once densely wooded nature of the dale. Some houses still have the remains of outside staircases, a once common feature of Scandinavian farm houses.

B Viewpoint of Central Swaledale.

C Muker village. A cluster of stone houses and one pub. Richard and Cherry Kearton, who were early wildlife photographers and lecturers in the late 19th and early 20th centuries, were born at Thwaite and went to school in Muker. Working without the advantage of modern film and telephoto lenses, they had to resort to such ingenious disguises as hiding inside a stuffed cow, or artificial tree trunks in order to get their desired shots.

Walk 3
KISDON HILL
4¼ miles (6.8 km) Moderate

0   1 mile

0   1 km

Kisdon Hill's grassy bulk dominates the head of Swaledale and its circuit offers a high-level panoramic ramble, with delightful views of the surrounding heather moors. The walk is from Keld, the highest village in the dale, and is approached by a side road off the B6270. Park in the village but take care not to block access to private property. The name Keld is the modern version of Kelda, which is Old Norse for a spring. Following the decline of lead mining in the late 19th century, the village lost the major portion of its population and has never recovered.

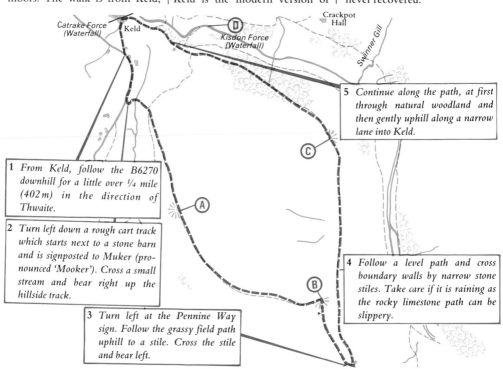

5 Continue along the path, at first through natural woodland and then gently uphill along a narrow lane into Keld.

1 From Keld, follow the B6270 downhill for a little over ¼ mile (402 m) in the direction of Thwaite.

2 Turn left down a rough cart track which starts next to a stone barn and is signposted to Muker (pronounced 'Mooker'). Cross a small stream and bear right up the hillside track.

3 Turn left at the Pennine Way sign. Follow the grassy field path uphill to a stile. Cross the stile and bear left.

4 Follow a level path and cross boundary walls by narrow stone stiles. Take care if it is raining as the rocky limestone path can be slippery.

A Viewpoint. The complex field patterns with their tiny stone barns are a typical feature of Upper Swaledale. Angram, a cluster of roadside farms, is directly across the valley.

B Viewpoint. This is considered by many to be one of the finest views in the Yorkshire Dales. Swaledale cuts a deep lush swathe through the rolling heather moors. Muker is directly below – a cluster of snug houses and farms in this exposed valley.

C Viewpoint. Swinner Gill, a one-time area of intensive lead mining, is opposite. Crackpot Hall is to the left of the deep-cut valley, ruined since rival interests undermined its foundations.

D Attractive waterfalls are another feature of Upper Swaledale. A signposted path, to the right of the walk, leads down to Kisdon Force. Closer to Keld, East Gill Force is in a pretty tree-lined hollow. Catrake, Currack and Wain Wath Forces are upstream from the village on either side of Park Bridge.

14

Walk 4
GUNNERSIDE GILL
6 miles (9.7 km) Moderate

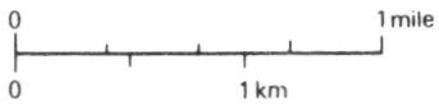

The upper part of Gunnerside Gill was once the scene of intensive lead mining and the extensive ruins of crushing plant and smelt mills are a poignant reminder of an industry which died out in Swaledale about 100 years ago.

The walk starts and finishes in the Swaledale village of Gunnerside, where there are parking facilities, and follows a route above the west side of Gunnerside Gill valley to reach the mining ground. The return is along the wooded east side. The route follows part of an historical nature trail and descriptive leaflets are on sale in Gunnerside. The village is named after the first Norse settler, Gunnar, who used the highland pastures for his livestock.

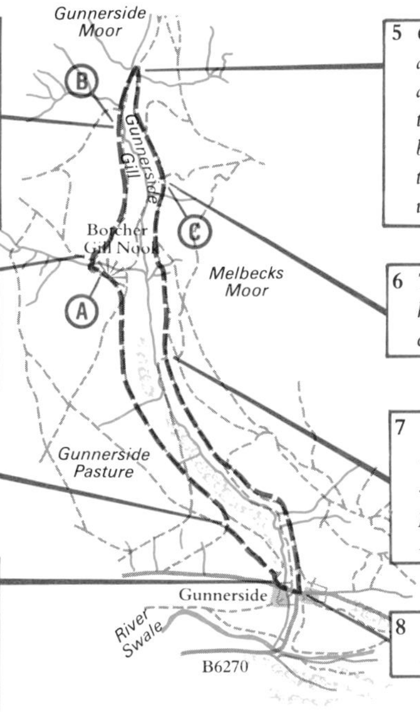

4 *Go to the right, downhill on a wide grassy path. Cross the rocky stream bed and climb, bearing right past a group of ruined buildings.* **Do not enter as the walls are crumbling with age.**

3 *Walk round the sharp bend above Botcher Gill. Then leave the track by turning right, onto a narrow path across the heather moor.*

2 *Turn right along a well-defined track, out to the open moors.*

1 *Take the upper and minor road, west out of Gunnerside. Cross a cattle grid and turn half right, uphill. The path is indistinct but part of the way follows the groove of an old track.*

5 *Cross the main stream by awkwardly placed stepping stones above a small waterfall. Climb up to another set of ruined mine buildings and then turn right past them. Start to walk down the valley.*

6 *Take the right fork down a spoil heap and pass an extensive group of mine buildings.*

7 *Take the left fork and keep slightly above the river-bank. Cross a stile and follow the undulating path through natural woodland. Follow yellow waymarks.*

8 *The path enters the village directly opposite the King's Head Inn.*

Map labels: Gunnerside Moor; (B); Gunnerside Gill; Botcher Gill Noop; (C); Melbecks Moor; (A); Gunnerside Pasture; Gunnerside; River Swale; B6270

A Viewpoint. Botcher Gill and its attractive waterfall are below the level of the track.

B The ruined buildings once housed crushing plant and above them is an old kiln used for drying the lead ore.

C Scree slopes on the valley sides were caused by a process known as 'hushing'. Water held back by temporary dams was released to scour the hillside and reveal the underlying rock. Mine entrances dot the hillside. **Do not enter any of them as they are danger-** ous but look for pieces of quartz and ore samples on the nearby spoil heaps. A locally available leaflet explains the history of lead mining in Swaledale.

Walk 5
SEMER WATER
4 miles (6.4 km) Easy

The walk is from Bainbridge, a Wensleydale village between Aysgarth and Hawes. Park in the village above a sloping green, seemingly undisturbed by traffic on this busy stretch of the A684. An easy path away from Bainbridge is followed by a mile (1.6 km) of road walking which leads to Countersett, where Semer Water is first revealed (see point C). From the lake, the return is beside and then above the River Bain all the way back to Bainbridge.

A Bainbridge. After the Norman Conquest, Bainbridge was the headquarters of the Wardens of the Forest of Wensleydale, who were entrusted with guarding it and its game in the name of the king. Their responsibility for law and order changed with the expansion of farmland and subsequent woodland clearance. The only tangible link with that ancient forest, which once covered this part of Wensleydale, is the custom of blowing a horn at 9pm every night from late September to Shrovetide, in order to guide travellers down from the fells.

B Viewpoint. The broad sweep of Upper Wensleydale stretches beyond Hawes and towards the blue hazy outlines of the Mallerstang Fells in the west.

C Viewpoint. The first glimpse of Semer Water in its moorland setting is revealed near a farmhouse as the road begins to descend.

D Viewpoint. Countersett, a village with long-standing Quaker traditions. 'Sett' is a common ending to place names in this part of Wensleydale. It comes from the Old Norse word 'sætre', which means a permanent or lowland farm-stead.

E Semer Water. The lake is a unique occurrence in the limestone dales. It owes its formation to a bed of impervious slate and a natural dam created by moraine, or debris, left by a retreating glacier. The lake is filled by rivers and streams draining a huge area of moorland to the south-west and, as a result, tiny River Bain, the only outlet for this water, is prone to flash floods, when the lake and river rise with alarming rapidity.

Semer Water has a romantic legend which speaks of a drowned village beneath its waters. The story tells of a traveller who tried to find shelter in the village one wild and stormy night but was refused by all except a poor shepherd and his wife whose house stood beyond the village. The next morning the traveller laid a curse, saying:

'Semer Water rise, Semer Water sink
And swallow all the town
Save yon little house
Where they gave me food and drink'.

Immediately after this curse was laid, a tremendous deluge caused the lake to rise suddenly and drown the village together with all its inhabitants, except for the shepherd and his wife. Strange as it may seem, a Bronze Age village was found when the lake level was lowered as part of a land reclamation scheme in 1937. Perhaps this legend is a piece of folk memory which has lingered for thousands of years.

Another legend surrounds the large boulder above the pebbly 'beach' near the road; this is the Carlow Stone, reputed to have been thrown there by the devil.

F Viewpoint. Wensleydale is below, its lushness contrasting with the moorland heights of Askrigg Common which fill the skyline. A flat-topped mound on a hillock to the right of Bainbridge is the site of the Roman fort of Virosidum. The outpost fortress guarded an area populated by wild tribespeople in Roman times. The Romans came here to exploit the lead ore found beneath nearby fells but would have needed the fort's protection against hostile local Venutian tribespeople. The Roman road from Ingleton to Bainbridge crosses Whether Hill and Cam Fell and part of it is followed on Walk 39 (Cam End and Ling Gill).

over

1 *Follow the cul-de-sac road away from the village green, past the Dame's School cottage and then along a private drive marked with a footpath sign. Climb away from the house, to the right, and into open fields.*

2 *Keep to the right of the large house as indicated by signposts and then cross the dip of the next field.*

3 *Go through the stile to the right of the barn and turn left along the road.*

4 *Bear left through Countersett and follow the road downhill to Semer Water.*

5 *Go through the narrow stile on the left next to the triple-arched bridge and follow the riverside path signposted to Bainbridge. Keep to the river-bank.*

6 *Climb a ladder stile and bear right uphill. Keep well to the left of the road and follow occasional waymark posts.*

7 *Join the side road and follow it down to the main road. Turn left into Bainbridge.*

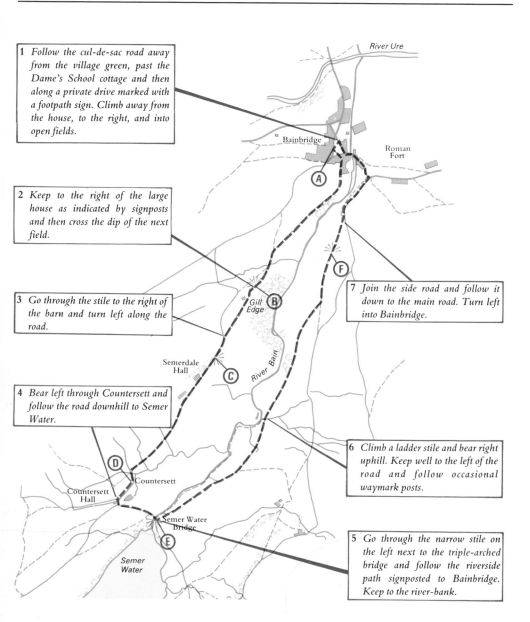

17

Walk 6
MARRICK PRIORY
5½ miles (8.9 km) Easy/moderate; one climb of 492 feet (150 m)

To reach the start of the walk, park your car in Reeth, in central Swaledale. Access to the village is by the B6270 from Richmond or along unclassified moorland roads from Leyburn or Aysgarth in Wensleydale. An alternative road follows Arkengarthdale south-east from the wild moors surrounding Tan Hill. Enjoy the facilities of Reeth before you walk down to Reeth Bridge and join the field path which eventually leads to Marrick Priory. Lush meadows, which are crossed beyond the priory, and a riverside stroll lead back to Reeth.

A Reeth. The village is built around a wide sloping green. Once the centre of lead mining in the area, its only links with that now dead industry are preserved in the Swaledale Folk Museum to the right of the village green. Other exhibits range from a collection of early farming implements to Swaledale's historical links with early Methodist preachers, who brought the Nonconformist faith to this remote area. As an indication of its earlier importance, Reeth at one time had a weekly market, held every Friday since its charter in 1695 and there were nine fairs throughout the year. A little over 100 years ago, at the height of the lead mining boom in Swaledale, the population of Reeth was about four times that of today. Nowadays, Reeth relies very much on tourism for its prosperity; pubs, restaurants and cafés offer a choice of refreshment with shops, an art gallery and local pottery of interest.

Being at the junction of Arkengarthdale with Swaledale has made Reeth an important focal point for Dales' farmers. Sheep sales are a regular event and the well-attended Reeth Agricultural Show and Sheepdog Trials takes place every August. Brass band concerts, another local tradition, are occasionally held on the village green.

B Viewpoint, looking along Swaledale towards its moorland headwaters.

C Viewpoint. The heather moors on the opposite side of the dale are stocked with grouse on behalf of shooting syndicates. Grinton Lodge, the castellated building set amidst sheltering trees beside the Leyburn road, was once a shooting lodge but is now a comfortable youth hostel.

D Steps Wood. There are reputed to be 365 steps leading down to the priory. They are known locally as the Nun's Steps and were built to connect Marrick Priory with farms and the village on the sunny plateau above this point.

E Marrick Priory. The 12th-century Benedictine Nunnery to the rear of the group of farm buildings is now used partly as a church and partly as a field study centre. The building is unusual in that it was undamaged during the Dissolution of the Monasteries in 1536, possibly because of the strong-willed nuns, who held out for five years before abandoning their secluded convent to the officers of Henry VIII. The priory and its attendant farm buildings are only changed by the passing of time.

The artist, Turner, visited Marrick Priory on his journeys through the Dales and forded the Swale at this point. If you do not mind getting your feet wet and you are sure the river is not too high, it is possible to extend the walk by crossing the river and following a right of way, across the B6270 to Hags Gill Farm. From the farm, a track climbs between two plantations out onto the moors surrounding Bleaberry Hill. The moor's boundary wall makes a safe guide, to the right, into Cogden Gill valley and, from there, an easy field path leads to Grinton. The route can be rejoined on the opposite side of Grinton Bridge (pointer no.10) for the return to Reeth.

over

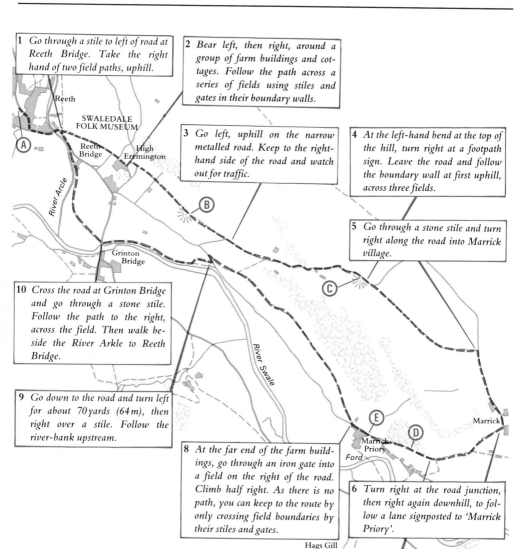

1 Go through a stile to left of road at Reeth Bridge. Take the right hand of two field paths, uphill.

2 Bear left, then right, around a group of farm buildings and cottages. Follow the path across a series of fields using stiles and gates in their boundary walls.

3 Go left, uphill on the narrow metalled road. Keep to the right-hand side of the road and watch out for traffic.

4 At the left-hand bend at the top of the hill, turn right at a footpath sign. Leave the road and follow the boundary wall at first uphill, across three fields.

5 Go through a stone stile and turn right along the road into Marrick village.

10 Cross the road at Grinton Bridge and go through a stone stile. Follow the path to the right, across the field. Then walk beside the River Arkle to Reeth Bridge.

9 Go down to the road and turn left for about 70 yards (64 m), then right over a stile. Follow the river-bank upstream.

8 At the far end of the farm buildings, go through an iron gate into a field on the right of the road. Climb half right. As there is no path, you can keep to the route by only crossing field boundaries by their stiles and gates.

6 Turn right at the road junction, then right again downhill, to follow a lane signposted to 'Marrick Priory'.

7 Continue by field path, then down through the wood on a flight of stone steps.

19

Walk 7
THE WATERFALLS OF AYSGARTH AND WEST BURTON
4¾ miles (7.6 km) Easy

```
0                                                    1 mile
|--------|--------|--------|--------|--------|
0                              1 km
```

West Burton is a little over a mile (1.6 km) to the south of Aysgarth. A series of waterfalls fills the tiny gorge below West Burton and, although just as attractive as their more famous sisters on either side of Aysgarth's mill bridge, these falls are almost unknown. This walk visits both sets of falls and provides the opportunity of comparing their merits. From the National Park car park north of the bridge, the walk is through fields to West Burton, then back via a footpath along the south bank and less frequented section of the Ure.

To reach the car park and Information Centre at Aysgarth, leave the A684 by driving down the Carperby road.

1 Cross the bridge and climb the flight of stone steps to the church. Continue along a narrow lane to the main road.

2 Cross the A684 and through the stile opposite. Across the fields, using stiles in their boundaries, until you reach Eshington Bridge.

3 Join the B6160 and cross the bridge. Turn right along a field path, signposted to West Burton.

4 Go left and right by road through the village.

5 Follow the lane from the lower part of the green, signposted to The Waterfall. Cross the narrow stone bridge. Then, by path, go left and right uphill.

6 Continue ahead as signposted to Barrack Wood, then left by woodland path.

7 Turn left down the farm lane and then right by a field path signposted to Edgley. Waymarked stiles and gates mark the route.

8 Turn right along the road for about 130 yards (120 m), then left through a gate into the last field on the left. Go diagonally left across the field to the main road.

9 Turn left over Hestholme Bridge and right by a waymarked path on its far side. Follow the riverbank to Aysgarth church.

A Follow the nature trail and woodland walks to the Middle and Lower Falls. Access to the falls is signposted from the car park. Also visit the Carriage Museum in the Old Corn Mill. High Force is upstream of the mill bridge. Spring is the time for this walk, especially after heavy rain when the woods and flowers are at their best and the falls at their most spectacular.

B West Burton is built around a wide village green. You can still see the smithy and the Fox & Hounds Inn is to the right of the renovated stocks. A curious spire takes the place of a more conventional preaching cross.

C Viewpoint. West Burton's waterfall from the footbridge.

D Twin stone follies on higher ground, off the path to the right, were built by lead miners around 1860. One looks like a pepper pot and was used for smoking bacon.

E Viewpoint. Lower and Middle Falls in their woodland setting.

Walk 8
ASKRIGG
5 miles (8 km) Easy/moderate; one climb of 531 feet (162 m)

Here is a fell and riverside walk from a village which will be easily recognised by followers of the *All Creatures Great & Small* TV series. Askrigg has been used on many occasions as the background to episodes in this popular television programme. The village is on the north side of Wensleydale and is easily approached from the A684, by way of Bainbridge or Worton. There is a small car park at the beginning of the walk.

1 *Follow the Muker road uphill and, a few yards beyond the last houses, go through a stile on the right marked with a signpost pointing to Newbiggin.*

2 *Cross the tiny green in Newbiggin; walk past a couple of houses and go through a farm gate. Bear left towards the lower of two stiles.*

Follow the waymarked path uphill and go through a small wood behind a group of barns.

3 *Turn right along the moorland lane, then left at a track junction above the large house. Follow the boundary wall.*

A

Newbiggin

Askrigg

B

6 *Go down a farm drive on the left, then right of the farm buildings to reach the river-bank. Turn right and follow the river upstream.*

D

Worton Bridge

C

Woodhall

River Ure

West End Farm

7 *Cross the road above Worton Bridge and then go half-right on a field path. Cross the railway track to reach Askrigg. Follow the lane and enter the main street opposite the church.*

5 *Go through the farmyard at West End and half right towards a metal gate. Go through it and over three fields. Then bear left down to the old railway track. Turn right to walk beside the track.*

4 *Keep right, downhill, along a cart track into the hamlet of Woodhall. Cross the main road and go down the lane opposite.*

A Viewpoint of Upper Wensleydale to the west, with the high fells bordering North Yorkshire and Cumbria.

B Viewpoint. The dale below this point was flooded in post glacial times by a moraine dam sited near modern Aysgarth. The dam held back a huge lake until it eventually burst under the pressure of water.

C Flagstones indicate that the footpath was once an important link between Askrigg and Worton.

D Askrigg. Cobbled frontages are an interesting feature of this attractive village of sturdy gritstone houses. The church is plain but pleasing, built mainly in the 17th and 18th centuries, no doubt on the site of an earlier version. Skeldale House, which is now an old peoples' home, is occasionally used as James Herriot's surgery in the TV series.

MAIDEN CASTLE
5 miles (8 km) Moderate

Do not expect to find the romantic ruins of a Norman stronghold when you reach Maiden Castle. Only the bare outlines of prehistoric earth-works are visible. However, it is the view of Swaledale which is the key feature of the walk. It starts from Grinton at the junction of the Leyburn and Redmire roads with the B6270. Rough moorland walking in the early part of the route contrasts with a gentle stroll back to Grinton beside the Swale. There is limited roadside parking in the village. Take care not to block access to drives .or field gates.

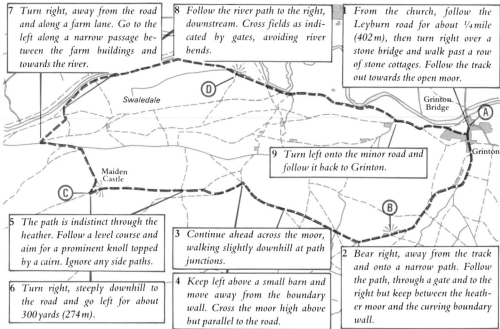

7 Turn right, away from the road and along a farm lane. Go to the left along a narrow passage between the farm buildings and towards the river.

8 Follow the river path to the right, downstream. Cross fields as indicated by gates, avoiding river bends.

1 From the church, follow the Leyburn road for about ¼ mile (402 m), then turn right over a stone bridge and walk past a row of stone cottages. Follow the track out towards the open moor.

Swaledale

Grinton Bridge

Grinton

9 Turn left onto the minor road and follow it back to Grinton.

Maiden Castle

5 The path is indistinct through the heather. Follow a level course and aim for a prominent knoll topped by a cairn. Ignore any side paths.

3 Continue ahead across the moor, walking slightly downhill at path junctions.

2 Bear right, away from the track and onto a narrow path. Follow the path, through a gate and to the right but keep between the heather moor and the curving boundary wall.

6 Turn right, steeply downhill to the road and go left for about 300 yards (274 m).

4 Keep left above a small barn and move away from the boundary wall. Cross the moor high above but parallel to the road.

A Grinton. Its pub is conveniently near the road junction. St. Andrews, opposite, is a later adaptation of a Norman church and is justifiably known as the 'Cathedral of the Dales'. At one time, it held the only consecrated burial ground in Swaledale and corpses had to be carried to it in special baskets for distances of up to 12 miles (19 km). An interesting feature of St. Andrew's is its leper's squint in the south wall, through which people with this dreadful disease could watch the service.

B Viewpoint of Central Swaledale. Grinton is below, then Reeth across the river with Arkengarthdale cleaving the northern moors.

C Maiden Castle viewpoint looking directly upstream along Swaledale. Roman relics found nearby hint that there was a battle between them and the British tribesmen holding Maiden Castle. Further excavations, locally, suggest that this part of Swaledale was a major settlement in the Bronze and Iron Ages.

D Viewpoint of ancient cultivation terraces above the valley road to the left of Reeth village.

Walk 10
HARDRAW FORCE
3½ miles (5.6 km) Easy

0   1 mile

0   1 km

Hardraw Force, England's highest above-ground waterfall is the highlight of this pleasant rural stroll.

The starting point for the walk is from the National Park Information Centre at Hawes car park, in the old station yard. Part of the Pennine Way route is then followed across Wensleydale to Hardraw village. After visiting the falls, a quiet field path climbs to Sedbusk village before returning to busy Hawes. A visit to the Information Centre, also the Upper Dales Folk Museum and possibly the nearby Rope Works, is highly recommended.

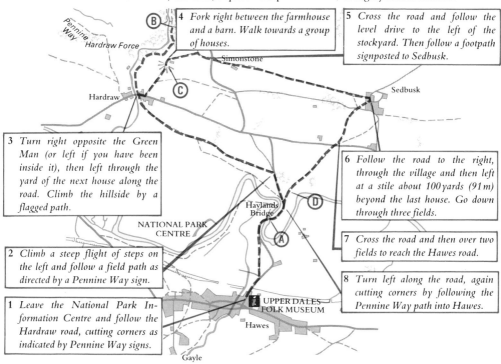

4 *Fork right between the farmhouse and a barn. Walk towards a group of houses.*

5 *Cross the road and follow the level drive to the left of the stockyard. Then follow a footpath signposted to Sedbusk.*

3 *Turn right opposite the Green Man (or left if you have been inside it), then left through the yard of the next house along the road. Climb the hillside by a flagged path.*

6 *Follow the road to the right, through the village and then left at a stile about 100 yards (91 m) beyond the last house. Go down through three fields.*

2 *Climb a steep flight of steps on the left and follow a field path as directed by a Pennine Way sign.*

7 *Cross the road and then over two fields to reach the Hawes road.*

8 *Turn left along the road, again cutting corners by following the Pennine Way path into Hawes.*

1 *Leave the National Park Information Centre and follow the Hardraw road, cutting corners as indicated by Pennine Way signs.*

A The river is the Ure, a shortened version of Yore, the old name for Wensleydale.

B Hardraw Force. The path enters Hardraw village directly opposite the Green Man Inn. Go through the bar, first paying a small toll and then out into the wooded gorge leading to the waterfall. The word 'force' is from the Norse 'foss', a waterfall. Bands sometimes play beneath the natural rocky amphitheatre.

C Viewpoint of Hardraw village and Upper Wensleydale. The Pennine Way leaves the village by the long lane climbing Great Shunner Fell to your right.

D The attractive stone bridge near a clump of trees in the last field prior to the Hawes road is probably on the line of an ancient green road linking villages on the north side of Swaledale. Lady Anne Clifford, Countess of Pembroke, an indefatigable 17th-century Dales' traveller, came this way after the Civil War to inspect her war-damaged properties.

Walk 11
CAM ROAD AND THE PENNINE WAY
6 miles (9.7 km) Moderate/strenuous; one climb of 1116 feet (340 m)

Two ancient tracks which converge on Hawes are followed by this walk. The first, Cam Road, is an old drove road, one of the many green roads which criss-cross the Yorkshire Dales. No longer used for transporting cattle and sheep to Midland markets, it now serves as a convenient track for local farmers to reach the high moorland pastures as well as being a pleasant walker's path. The second is a delightful grassy track now followed by the Pennine Way long-distance footpath. Originally, the path was a more direct link between Cam Road and Hawes. It was also used as an access track to reach the peat-gathering grounds at Ten End. Ten End is the junction point for both tracks and the inward turning point for the walk. Car parking should be easy

to find at either end of Hawes.

Hawes is a busy market town, the 'capital' of Upper Wharfedale and a useful base for exploring the dales to the north. The word Hawes comes from a Norse word 'haus', meaning a pass or gap. It is sometimes corrupted as 'house', and occurs throughout the Northern Pennines and the Lake District. Hawes no longer has a railway but the old station buildings have been put to good use as the Yorkshire Dales National Park Information Centre and also the Upper Dales Folk Museum. The latter houses a collection of farm equipment and records of the area's past, made by two Daleswomen. At one time, hand knitting was an important secondary industry to farming but the only remaining traditional hand craft in Wensleydale is rope-

making. In a shed at the entrance to the station car park, the 200-year-old method of hand twisting short ropes is demonstrated. The ropes are used for cattle or horse halters. The famous Wensleydale cheese is made at the nearby dairy, to traditionally high standards but by modern methods.

Before starting out on the walk, look at the plaque above the door of the house opposite the telephone kiosks. Obviously strong supporters of the Commonwealth which followed the Civil War, the original owners ask the unanswerable question:

'God being with us
who can be against?'

The date over the plaque is 1668 but we do not know who built the house, other than his initials, which were T.A.F.

A Cam Road. This is one of the 'green roads' which have criss-crossed the Dales since time immemorial. Cam Road is a link with Cam High Road which it joins in the south-west at Kidhow Gate. Cam High Road is Roman in origin and can be traced from Ingleton to Bainbridge. Parts of its surface are metalled but, as with Cam Road, it runs for miles across the moors as a high-level track. Once used by drovers and local travellers, the track is freely available to walkers and horse riders.

B Viewpoint. The little side dale

of Snaizeholme Beck is below and the bold outline of Ingleborough rises beyond the dale head.

C The path, from Ten End, is part of the 270-mile (435 km) Pennine Way footpath which links Edale in Derbyshire with Kirk Yetholm in the Scottish Borders. Even though the moorland path is easy to follow at this point, prominent cairns also indicate its route.

D Viewpoint. Wensleydale is below. The Pennine Way crosses the dale beyond Hawes and climbs the broad shoulder of

Great Shunner Fell away to your left.

E Viewpoint. Gayle, the village in front and to the right, is worth a few minutes diversion. Attractive cottages line the roads on either side of the stepped waterfalls of Gayle Beck. The village was founded by Vikings who built on the foundations of a Celtic settlement.

F Notice the curious little spire which has been added, almost as an afterthought, to one corner of the tower of Hawes church.

over

0 _____ 1 mile

0 _____ 1 km

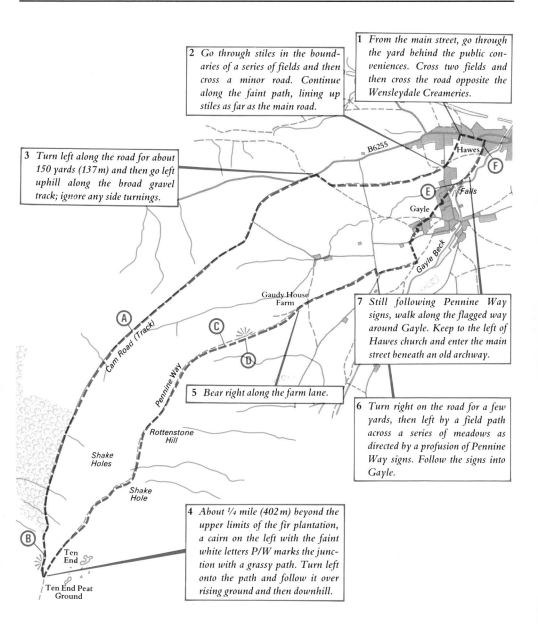

1 From the main street, go through the yard behind the public conveniences. Cross two fields and then cross the road opposite the Wensleydale Creameries.

2 Go through stiles in the boundaries of a series of fields and then cross a minor road. Continue along the faint path, lining up stiles as far as the main road.

3 Turn left along the road for about 150 yards (137 m) and then go left uphill along the broad gravel track; ignore any side turnings.

B6255

Hawes

F

E

Falls

Gayle

Gayle Beck

Gaudy House Farm

A

Cam Road (Track)

C

D

Pennine Way

7 Still following Pennine Way signs, walk along the flagged way around Gayle. Keep to the left of Hawes church and enter the main street beneath an old archway.

5 Bear right along the farm lane.

6 Turn right on the road for a few yards, then left by a field path across a series of meadows as directed by a profusion of Pennine Way signs. Follow the signs into Gayle.

Rottenstone Hill

Shake Holes

Shake Hole

B

Ten End

Ten End Peat Ground

4 About ¼ mile (402 m) beyond the upper limits of the fir plantation, a cairn on the left with the faint white letters P/W marks the junction with a grassy path. Turn left onto the path and follow it over rising ground and then downhill.

Walk 12
HELL GILL
4¾ miles (7.6 km) Moderate

The final upper limits of Wensleydale end in the wild, little-known moors of Mallerstang Common and the walk is in this region as far as Hell Gill on the boundary of North Yorkshire with Cumbria. To reach the start of the walk, drive north-west along the B6259 (Kirkby Stephen road) for about a mile (1.6 km) beyond the Moorcock Inn; there is limited roadside parking and there are lay-bys between Shotlock tunnel and the prominent forest at Lunds.

5 *Cross the bridge and turn left, down the farm track. Cross the railway bridge and continue to the road.*

4 *Climb a stone stile and turn left along the moorland track.*

2 *Follow a signposted footpath to Shaws, the tree-sheltered white house high on the hillside.*

The High Way

Hell Gill Bridge

Hellgill

Shaws

3 *Turn left over the bridge. Then bear right above the house. Follow a faint path up the hillside.*

9 *Keep above the portal of Shotlock tunnel. Go through the gate and turn right along the road.*

8 *Keep level across the pathless moor for about ¼ mile (402 m). Then descend gradually to the left, towards the railway tunnel.*

Aisgill Moor Cottages

Shotlock Tunnel

The Quarry

High Shaw Paddock

6 *Cross the road. Then go through a gate and turn left. There is no path, so follow the moorland boundary wall.*

7 *Go half right through the abandoned farm-yard and, still following the boundary wall, aim for the gate in the corner of the next field.*

1 *Walk down the road, away from the forest, to a footpath sign near the Quarry. Turn left across a rough field and go through the pine wood. Turn right along the forest drive.*

A The abandoned simple stone chapel, to the right of the path, once served this scattered moorland community.

B Shaws stands above a narrow ravine filled by an attractive natural water garden.

C The track is an old coach road called the High Way which formerly linked York and Carlisle. The track mostly follows the north side of Wensleydale and, in places, it is difficult to trace but, in its lower reaches below Askrigg, it is now the basis of the modern road.

D Viewpoint. The moors of Mallerstang Common are opposite; Wild Boar Fell is the highest point – 2323 feet (708 m) – and Aisgill waterfall can usually be seen close to the railway line.

E Sturdy Hell Gill Bridge was built to last, once carrying coaches and horses as well as driven cattle. Look over the parapet on either side into the deep chasm created by the stream wearing its way through a section of softer limestone.

F Aisgill summit is the highest point on the Settle to Carlisle line, where steam trains are run frequently.

26

Walk 13
DENTDALE
6 miles (9.7 km) Moderate

```
0                                                1 mile
|_____|_____|_____|_____|_____|
0                      1 km
```

The walk explores central Dent dale from Dent, a charming village of cobbled streets and a jumble of stone cottages sur- rounding a sturdy church. Adam Sedgwick, the father of modern geology, was born in Dent. The link is commemorated by an imposing granite monolith in the main street. Parking space can be found at the western (Sedbergh) end of the village.

11 *Turn right at the signpost pointing to a shady path, then left at the road and follow it back over Church Bridge into Dent.*

10 *Turn left on the footpath signposted to Tommy Bridge. Cross the footbridge and turn left downstream.*

9 *Turn right along the lane and right at the junction with the valley road.*

8 *Cross the access drive and bear left in front of the farm. Follow a line of trees out towards the open fields. Then go downhill to the road next to a ruined barn.*

1 *Go down the main road, past the church and towards the river. Do not cross the bridge but turn right to follow the side stream.*

2 *Go left, over a wooden footbridge and then right, still following the path upstream.*

3 *Go past the farmhouse and left over a stile to follow a field boundary as far as a path junction. Turn right and follow a gravel path up to the road.*

4 *Cross the road at Bridge End and follow the woodland path as indicated by signposts. Continue by field paths.*

5 *Do not climb as far as the old farmhouse but bear left, closer to the river-bank. There is no path but stiles mark the way.*

6 *Turn left across a footbridge below the stone barn. Walk downstream for a few yards, then bear right uphill along a leafy lane to a farm. Go to the right through the farm-yard.*

7 *Turn sharp left in front of a low stone building. Climb the steep bank and go over a stile at its top. Walk towards Rigg End Farm.*

A Dentdale is the 'border territory' between the Yorkshire Dales and the Lake District. Its character and architecture are different to the more easterly dales, but they are also not of Lakeland; Dentdale has a unique atmosphere.

B The small round tower-like object at the side of the path is not a fortification but a derelict limekiln.

C Viewpoint. The massive bulk of Whernside, 2525 feet (736 m), blocks the head of Deepdale.

D Whernside Manor. This is the Yorkshire Dales National Park Outdoor Study and Recreation Centre where activity holidays of all grades are held.

E Viewpoint. Dent, with its parish church in the foreground and backcloth of Crag Hill, makes an attractive photographic subject.

Walk 14
WINDER

4¾ miles (7.6 km) Strenuous; one climb of 112 feet (34 m)

As the Matterhorn is to Zermatt, so Winder is to Sedbergh. Boys from Sedbergh School sing of their love for Winder and the friendly protection it offers by sheltering their town from the north winds. The 'i', incidentally, is short as in 'window'. To the town, Winder is simply 'The Fell', special to the inhabitants though only an outlier of the glorious rolling hills known as the Howgills. This little-known mass of delectable hills is usually seen, though only fleetingly, by travellers on the M6 or Carlisle to London trains. The walk is from Sedbergh, a town built on a southern slope between the Howgill Fells and the River Rawthey; parking can usually be found in the town centre.

As the walk is in open country, it is only suitable for a clear day. Please note that the path beyond the farm at pointer no.3 and the one across the summit of Winder are not rights of way but walkers are normally permitted to use them.

5 Continue ahead and downhill along the grassy ridge to a broad col.

4 Follow the wall above a pinewood and turn right on a steeply inclined path towards the rounded summit of Winder.

6 Turn right, again downhill, following a well-made path.

7 Go downhill as far as the intake gate at Lockbank Farm. Turn left away from the farm, again following the fell boundary wall.

8 Turn right through a kissing gate and walk downhill to the right of a shaley wooded gorge.

Winder

(B) (C)

Nursery Wood

(A)

3 Go half right through the farmyard, then left by the grassy path alongside the boundary wall.

Castlehaw Tower

Lockbank Farm

Motte & Bailey

(D)

2 Turn right and follow Howgill Lane to the end of the 30mph limit. Then turn right on a path marked 'To the Fell'. Walk up to Lockbank Farm.

Sedbergh

Sedbergh School

1 Turn right from the car park, then left along the High Street.

9 Follow the farm lane, to the right, into the outskirts of Sedbergh. The church and central car parks are on the right of the town centre.

A Viewpoint. Sedbergh is below with Garsdale and Dentdale winding towards the high eastern fells.

B Viewpoint. The panoramic all-round view takes in most of the highest Lakeland peaks; then south and east are Morecambe Bay and the valleys of the Lune, Dent and Garsdale in that order. In the background, you can see the rolling mass of the Howgills.

C Viewpoint. The Rawthey valley is below with Sedbergh tucked beneath the foot of Winder.

D It is possible to extend this walk by following Walk 15 (Sedbergh and the River Rawthey); the valley and riverside walk will make an interesting contrast to the ascent of Winder.

Walk 15
SEDBERGH AND THE RIVER RAWTHEY
4½ miles (7.2 km) Easy/moderate

Even though the pleasant market town of Sedbergh is 'officially' part of the Yorkshire Dales National Park, it has an atmosphere more akin to the Lake District than those towns and villages of the eastern dales. Shel-tered by the Howgill Fells to its north, Sedbergh has a sunny aspect and is fortunate in having the Rawthey, a fine trout river and a tributary of the Lune, on its doorstep. There are parking facilities in the town centre and access is via the A683 Kirkby Stephen road or the A684 from Wensleydale. From the M6, follow the A684 eastwards from Junction 37. This walk can be extended by joining it to Walk 14, which begins and ends in Sedbergh.

3 *Bear right at Castlehaw Farm into open fields. Keep to the left of the boundary wall but change sides at a stile next to a massive upright stone.*

4 *Turn right at Ghyll Farm and walk down the concrete lane.*

5 *Bear left around Stone Hall, go through a gate, turn left again and follow a boundary wall downhill.*

6 *Follow the field path to the right of Hollin Hill Farm.*

2 *Turn left to follow a narrow lane opposite the road junction.*

7 *Bear right at the side of the large white house and then walk down its access drive.*

1 *From the car park, walk to the right along Main Street for about 80 yards (73 m), passing the Information Centre.*

10 *Cross the Garsdale road and continue to follow the riverbank. Turn right with the path and climb past a school building, then beside the rugby field into Sedbergh. The town centre is to the left.*

8 *Follow yellow waymarks to the left through the stockyard at Buckbank. Follow the hedge downhill to the road bridge.*

9 *Cross the road, climb the stile and follow the riverside path downstream.*

A The double mound on the right is a Motte & Bailey, the remains of a stockade fort probably built in the 11th century.

B Viewpoint looking across the Rawthey Valley into Garsdale.

C Viewpoint. Frostow Fells are opposite above the confluence of Garsdale's Clough River and the Rawthey stream.

D Viewpoint. Sedbergh is to your left, backed by the mass of the Howgill Fells.

29

MIDDLEHAM
2½ miles (4km) Easy

Richard, Duke of Gloucester, Yorkist and future King Richard III (1452-1485), once lived in the imposing Norman Castle which still dominates Middleham. The small market town is at the junction of the A6108, Leyburn road and the minor road which runs along Coverdale to Kettlewell in Wharfedale. To join the walk, park near the market square.

The main walls of the castle date from 1170 when it became the property of the powerful Neville family but the massive and well-preserved Keep is the original, built by Robert Fitzralf, nephew of William the Conqueror. Its towering bulk remains a true memorial to the master masons who erected it more than eight centuries ago. The white boar crest of the hunchbacked King Richard can (with a little imagination) still be made out on top of the Swine Cross in the market square.

Another feature in the town is St. Alkelda's Well, the martyred Saxon princess who died at the hands of the Danes rather than renounce her Christian beliefs. It is her name to which the parish church is dedicated. In the market place and near the Swine Cross, there is a ring where bulls were once tied for the cruel sport of bull-baiting.

During his training to become a knight, Richard met and married Anne, the daughter of Richard Neville who was better known as Warwick the Kingmaker. Through Anne, he became owner of Middleham and spent many happy hours indulging in the royal sport of hunting game throughout the Dales. Edward, Richard's only legitimate son, was born in Middleham but died aged 12. His room can be seen in the castle ruins. King Richard, since his portrayal by Shakespeare in Richard III, has been looked upon as an evil king but recent research sees him otherwise. It is in this light that we can think of him as a lover of the Dales, especially Coverdale and his beloved Middleham Castle.

Middleham, the Newmarket of the North, is the centre of a bloodstock breeding area with a dozen or so trainers handling hundreds of potentially top-class racehorses. These fine animals are exercised on the wide expanse of Middleham Moor, to the north of the Coverdale road.

About a mile (1.6km) beyond Middleham towards Leyburn, the road crosses the River Ure by an imposing iron girder bridge, which was built by public subscription in 1850, replacing a suspension bridge which collapsed in 1831 after only two years' use. Below the town, in Swaledale, the River Ure, which is now joined by the Cover, widens as it reaches the broad acres of the Vale of York. The dale's character becomes more wooded in its flatter lower reaches. About 3 miles (4.8km) from Middleham along the Masham Road, you will find the ruins of Jervaulx Abbey. During the life of this abbey, the Cistercian monks who lived there became famous for their cheese, a forerunner of Wensleydale, but made from ewes' milk.

In 1536, the Pilgrimage of Grace started from Jervaulx, led by the abbot, Adam Sedbergh. His intention was to try to persuade Henry VIII against the dissolution of the monasteries but the pilgrimage failed and Jervaulx, along with countless others, was destroyed. Abbot Sedbergh and many of his followers were imprisoned in the Tower of London and executed at Tyburn in 1537.

A The imposing ruins of the castle are worth viewing from within and also from the lane end. When Richard III, having reigned for only two years, lost not only his horse and the Battle of Bosworth but also the Crown of England in 1485, his successor, Henry Tudor, had no wish to own Middleham. Along with the unhappy memories of his rival, it was abandoned and languished for 161 years. However, because it retained its obvious potential as a fortress, Cromwell's troops made it untenable in 1646, during the Civil War. Its ruins later became a free quarry for ready-dressed stones and many of the older houses in the town are probably built from materials

over

taken from the castle. The castle is now in the care of English Heritage.

B A mound which tops the rising field on the right predates the castle and is the earth base of an earlier timber fortification which was abandoned when the main castle was built.

C Hullo Bridge. Its stone arch speaks of its use by once heavier traffic than cattle or the occasional tractor and probably carried a coach road south across Coverdale to the interesting 17th-century house of Braithwaite Hall.

D The attractive pond on the left is a popular picnic spot. Horses can often be seen being exercised on the nearby common.

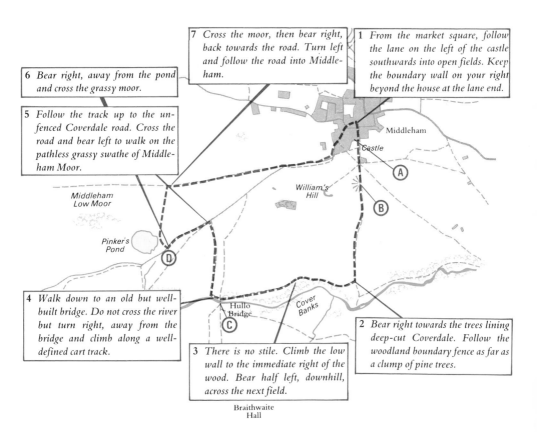

7 Cross the moor, then bear right, back towards the road. Turn left and follow the road into Middleham.

1 From the market square, follow the lane on the left of the castle southwards into open fields. Keep the boundary wall on your right beyond the house at the lane end.

6 Bear right, away from the pond and cross the grassy moor.

5 Follow the track up to the unfenced Coverdale road. Cross the road and bear left to walk on the pathless grassy swathe of Middleham Moor.

Middleham

Castle

A

Middleham Low Moor

William's Hill

B

Pinker's Pond

D

4 Walk down to an old but well-built bridge. Do not cross the river but turn right, away from the bridge and climb along a well-defined cart track.

Hullo Bridge

C

Cover Banks

2 Bear right towards the trees lining deep-cut Coverdale. Follow the woodland boundary fence as far as a clump of pine trees.

3 There is no stile. Climb the low wall to the immediate right of the wood. Bear half left, downhill, across the next field.

Braithwaite Hall

31

Walk 17
COVERDALE
4½ miles (7.2 km) Easy

This walk is in a quiet section of rural Coverdale. The paths are mainly those used by locals for their evening or Sunday afternoon strolls and provide a pleasant alternative to the better-known areas of the Yorkshire Dales.

The walk starts and finishes in Carlton. You can park near the Forester's Arms in this small farming village on the minor road linking Middleham and Kettlewell by way of steep Park Rash.

9 Turn right at the main road and immediately right again through a stile giving access to a field path into Carlton.

8 Walk uphill along the road. At a signpost to Carlton, turn right through a stone stile and climb through a series of fields using stiles in their boundary walls.

7 Keep to the right above Gilbert Scar Lodge and then walk down its access drive to the road. Turn left and cross the bridge.

6 Turn right and follow the lane into Swineside. Go through a gate behind the hotel and bear right, diagonally downhill through a series of fields. Use gates to follow the correct route.

1 From your parking place near the Forester's Arms, walk east away from the village centre. Turn right along narrow Quaker Lane, signposted to the River Cover and West Scrafton.

2 Follow the direction of a fingerpost to the right across meadowland.

3 Follow Goodman's Gill downstream and cross the River Cover by its twin footbridges.

4 Climb up the next field as far as a wooded side stream and then bear right onto a faint path across a series of fields leading to West Scrafton. Turn right through the village.

5 Turn left and walk along the road to Swineside.

Carlton
PH
Goodman's Gill
Ⓐ
Caygill Foot Bridge
Howden Gill
Ⓑ
West Scrafton
Ⓒ
Gilbert Scar Lodge
Coverdale
Ⓓ
Swineside

A Viewpoint of deep-cut Goodman's Gill and the main valley of Coverdale.

B Viewpoint. The long line of Carlton's sturdy cottages and farm houses line the opposite hillside.

C Holes in the garden wall of the end cottage in West Scrafton once held straw beehives. The name Scrafton means the 'town by the hollow' in Saxon and presumably Coverdale is the hollow. The village is a tight packed group of houses around a tiny village green, an ideal base for exploring the lesser-known fells surrounding Scrafton Moor and Great Haw.

D Viewpoint of Upper Coverdale, with Little Whernside on your left and Buckden Pike right.

Walk 18
BUCKDEN AND UPPER WHARFEDALE
5 miles (8 km) Easy; one climb of 360 feet (110 m)

From the picturesque village of Buckden in Upper Wharfedale, the route, which begins at Buckden car park, first climbs Buckden Rake by a track which was originally built by the Romans and later used as a coach road. Crossing the B6160 at Cray, a delightful high-level path next leads to Scar House Farm, from where a downhill track reaches the valley bottom. Finally, a simple riverside stroll leads back towards Buckden.

5 Turn left at the signpost, down through the farm-yard at Scar House and out along its access lane into the valley bottom.

4 Follow the track behind the White Lion Inn and then ahead on a level path beyond the last farm building.

3 Turn sharp left, downhill to Cray; cross the stream and then the road.

2 Walk forward at the signpost, along a level grassy path which follows the boundary wall.

1 Take the upward-slanting track away from Buckden car park, signposted to Buckden Pike and Cray.

6 Cross the bridge at Hubberholme, then left along the road for about ½ mile (0.8 km), passing the George Inn.

7 Go through a gate into a field on the left signposted to Buckden Bridge. Follow the boundary wall and then the river-bank as far as the road.

8 Turn left over the road bridge and walk uphill towards Buckden village green.

(Map labels: Cray, Scar House, Todd's Wood, Buckden Rake, Hubberholme, Buckden Lane, Buckden Wood, River Wharfe, Buckden, A, B, C, D, E, F)

A Viewpoint. The deep-cut limestone valley of Upper Wharfedale is to the right and left. The dale is followed by an unclassified road north over Langstroth Chase to Hawes and also by the Dales Way long distance footpath; the latter turns north-west to join the Cam High Road above Cam Pasture.

B Cray. An upland farming community, built here to take advantage of a line of springs for its water supply on these otherwise dry limestone fells. The White Lion, once a coaching inn, still makes a welcome stopping place.

C Viewpoint. Look down the deep wooded cleft of Crook Gill on the left of the path. The trees and shade-loving plants are the descendants of survivors of the last Ice Age which denuded the surrounding uplands.

D Viewpoint. Looking out from the limestone pavement to Buckden Pike on your left and the Hore Head moors above the western rim of Wharfedale.

E Viewpoint. The squat Church of St. Michael and All Saints is below in Hubberholme, a village named after Hubba, the original Viking settler in this area. The church is Norman and has a medieval loft painted in red and gold as well as modern woodwork by Robert Thompson of Kilburn; look for his 'church mouse' trademark. The George Inn is over the bridge from the church and was once the property of incumbent vicars.

33

Walk 19
HAWKSWICK MOOR
7 miles (11.3 km) Moderate/strenuous

Footpaths, which are centuries old, are used to connect the three villages and two dales visited on this walk. The paths date from a time long before roads designed to cope with wheeled traffic appeared in the Dales, a time when most people rarely travelled beyond their parish boundaries.

The first village, the point of departure for the walk, is Kettlewell in Wharfedale; the name is Old Norse and its meaning is either 'Kettil's Well', or 'Bubbling Spring'. Beyond Knife Scar,

the path descends into Littondale. This name differs from most of the other dales, except Wensleydale, in that it is not derived from the name of the river. In this case, the river is the Skirfare. Hawkswick is the next village, its name indicating that birds of prey once lived nearby. Arncliffe village also has similar links: although its name has no immediate apparent meaning, in translation from Old Norse, it means Eagles' Cliff.

Charles Kingsley stayed for a time in Arncliffe, when he was

writing his novel, 'The Water Babies', a book which condemned the Victorian practice of sending small boys up chimneys in order to sweep down the soot. He travelled widely throughout the Yorkshire Dales and his water babies' home was the pool at the foot of Malham Cove.

Park your car in Kettlewell. There is usually space near the bridge or along one of the village streets but be careful not to interfere with access to premises or block farm gates.

A Viewpoint. Look back towards Kettlewell. Its church is unusual in that it is built to one side of the village, rather than near the centre, inferring, perhaps, that the village has expanded westwards rather than outwards from a central point. The main road only touches the outskirts of the village. Most of the old cottages lining the side streets and alleys were once the homes of lead miners who worked beneath the nearby fells. Kettlewell was an important halt in the days of coaches and horses; its three inns date from that time. The main route from London to Richmond followed Wensleydale to Kettlewell, then climbed over the notoriously steep Park Rash to the north-east of the village, where passengers were expected to get out and push! Park Rash has been used as a hill-climb to test cars and motor-cycles.

B Viewpoint. Pastoral Wharfedale is ahead and contrasts with rockier and narrower Littondale to your right. Immediately below are the rough outlines of a prehistoric field system. People were able to live on these higher fells during a period when the climate was warmer than now.

C Viewpoint. Hawkswick and its sheltering belt of trees is below. The Skirfare flows gently by the village on its way to join the Wharfe at Amerdale Dub. Dubs are deep pools in rivers, usually the home of large trout.

D The route passes Arncliffe church. The rest of the village is to the left. It has one pub, the Falcon, and a tea room.

E Primroses, bluebells and woodland violets grow in profu-

sion every spring in Park Scar woods. Please leave them where they are: picking wild flowers spoils the enjoyment of other visitors and also it will often kill the parent plant.

F Viewpoint. Arncliffe is below amidst its ancient field patterns outlined by enclosure walls.

G Heather growing on the rocky fellside indicates that the soil is acidic and the surface rock is gritstone, capping the more common Dales' limestone, which is an alkaline rock. Native heather will only grow in an acid environment.

H Viewpoint. Kettlewell is framed in the lower portals of the rocky cleft in Gate Close Scar. Take care when following the path over its slippery rocks.

over

7 Climb the steep footpath sign-posted to Kettlewell. Go through a belt of mature woodland below the escarpment rocks.

8 The moorland path is indistinct in places. Look for a prominent signpost on the skyline pointing the way to the right, towards a clearer track.

9 Cross a well-defined cart track and continue downhill diagonally across the hillside on a grassy path. Go through a narrow rocky gully to reach the valley bottom.

10 Go through a gate and turn left at the road. Cross the bridge into Kettlewell village.

1 Follow the Threshfield road (B6160) out of Kettlewell for a little over a quarter of a mile (402 m). Turn right through a gate marked by a signpost to Hawkswick. Climb the rocky path across the sparsely wooded hillside.

2 Yellow waymarks indicate the route of the hillside path which becomes grassier as it gains height.

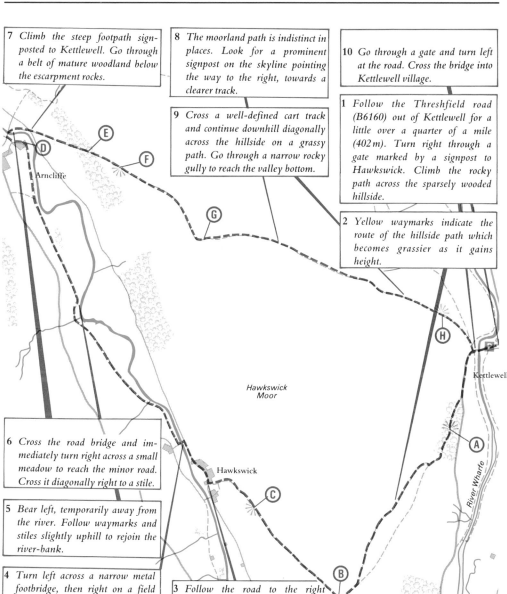

Arncliffe

Hawkswick Moor

Hawkswick

Kettlewell

River Wharfe

6 Cross the road bridge and im-mediately turn right across a small meadow to reach the minor road. Cross it diagonally right to a stile.

5 Bear left, temporarily away from the river. Follow waymarks and stiles slightly uphill to rejoin the river-bank.

4 Turn left across a narrow metal footbridge, then right on a field path. Follow the river upstream.

3 Follow the road to the right through Hawkswick.

Walk 20
KETTLEWELL AND STARBOTTON
4½ miles (7.2 km) Easy

Here is an easy, low-level walk connecting two attractive Upper Wharfedale villages. From Ket- tlewell on the B6160, a field path, which is centuries old, links it with Starbotton. The return is by a riverside path downstream along the Wharfe. There is a car park near the river in Kettlewell.

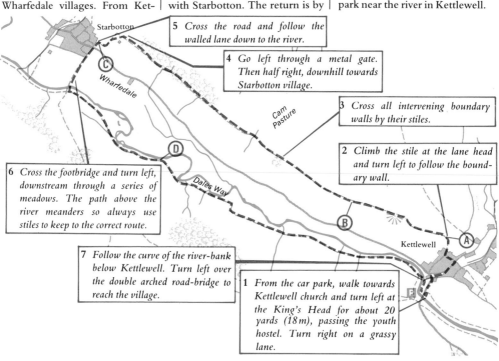

5 Cross the road and follow the walled lane down to the river.

4 Go left through a metal gate. Then half right, downhill towards Starbotton village.

3 Cross all intervening boundary walls by their stiles.

2 Climb the stile at the lane head and turn left to follow the bound- ary wall.

6 Cross the footbridge and turn left, downstream through a series of meadows. The path above the river meanders so always use stiles to keep to the correct route.

7 Follow the curve of the river-bank below Kettlewell. Turn left over the double arched road-bridge to reach the village.

1 From the car park, walk towards Kettlewell church and turn left at the King's Head for about 20 yards (18 m), passing the youth hostel. Turn right on a grassy lane.

A Viewpoint. Kettlewell fits snugly above the junction of Cam Gill Beck and the River Wharfe. The name Kettlewell is Old Norse and means either 'Bub- bling Spring' or 'Kettil's Well'.

B The smaller 'in-by' fields on the left are enclosed for use either as hay meadows or for breeding spring lambs. Larger fields on the right lead out towards the open upland grazing areas.

C Starbotton. The Fox & Hounds, a little way along the main road, makes a convenient half-way resting place on this walk. Starbotton is a corruption of Stannerbotton, Old Norse meaning 'the valley where the stakes were cut'.

D The riverside path is part of the Dales' Way long-distance path between Ilkley and Bowness on Lake Windermere. The route is along Wharfedale, then by way of the moors of Cam End and Gearstones into verdant Dent- dale. Beyond Dentdale, the path skirts the southern foot of the Howgill Fells and leaves North Yorkshire by crossing the Crook of Lune close to the M6. The Cumbrian section of the Dales' Way is through Burneside near Kendal and then over a range of low fells to the west of Staveley to reach Windermere at the end of what is considered the most sce- nically attractive of all the long- distance footpaths.

Walk 21
CONISTONE'S PASTURES

4¾ miles (7.6 km) Easy/moderate; one climb of 294 feet (90 m)

The quiet Wharfedale village of Conistone is about 3 miles (4.8 km) to the north-west of Grassington along an unclassified loop road off the B6160. The walk starts by rising gradually on grassy paths, almost into Grassington before returning partly along the Dales' Way and finally descends by a steep, narrow dry valley which leads directly back to Conistone. As roadside parking in the centre of Conistone is limited, take care not to block access to private property.

1 *From the centre of Conistone, walk along the Grassington road for 100 yards (91 m) past the Methodist chapel. Follow the cart track uphill on the left, signposted to Grassington.*

2 *Walk ahead on a grassy path following the direction of signposts.*

3 *Climb a stone stile and cross the grassy upper limits of the rocky gorge.*

4 *Turn left over a ladder stile across a stone wall. Gradually bear right over the rocky upland pastures. Keep well to the left of the woodland boundary until you reach a second boundary wall, at right angles to the path. Do not cross this wall.*

5 *At the boundary wall, within sight of Grassington, bear left and follow the grassy path.*

6 *The faint springy turf footpath continues across a series of upland pastures. Line up stiles and gates in the boundary walls.*

7 *Cross a stile and go left as indicated by the signpost to Conistone. Go downhill into the dry valley. Keep to the left and below the TV booster mast.*

8 *Follow the steadily narrowing rocky valley all the way to Conistone.*

Hut Circle Enclosures

Conistone

Field System

Settlements

Dales Way

Cairn

Bastow Wood

Site of Medieval Village

Field System

A Viewpoint of Grass Wood Nature Reserve and Bastow Wood on its left (Walk 22, Ghaistrill's Strid and Grass Wood, explores part of this nature reserve).

B Viewpoint. White Nook limestone gorge is below, where semi-alpine flowers such as rock rose, mountain pansy and wild thyme can be found.

C Hollows at the side of the path were trial holes in the search for lead. Extensive deposits of the ore were mined beneath Grassington Moor, further to the east of this point, until cheap imports killed off the industry towards the end of the last century.

D Viewpoint. Modern Grassington is ahead but nearby are the grassy outlines of a medieval village wiped out by the Black Death.

E Here, the walk follows part of the Dales' Way.

F Viewpoint. Bare rocky hillsides nearby are still denuded 10 to 12 thousand years after the last Ice Age.

37

Walk 22
GHAISTRILL'S STRID AND GRASS WOOD
4¼ miles (7.2 km) Easy/moderate

This walk is from Grassington, 'capital' of the Dales and headquarters of the Yorkshire Dales National Park, the body entrusted with the difficult task of preserving and enhancing the landscape, as well as protecting the livelihoods of people living and working within the boundaries of the park. The authority must also look after the amenity interests of the thousands of visitors who wish to enjoy this part of the English countryside.

Grassington is a small town with a mixture of architectural styles, including many fine Georgian dwellings, and, although it grew with the fortunes of nearby lead mines, its foundations are much older. The town suffered during the period of Scottish border raids in the 14th and later centuries but worse by far was the visitation of the Black Death plague in 1349, when over a quarter of the population in the vicinity of Grassington died.

The Upper Wharfedale Folk Museum of farming and local industry is in the town square. Adventure holidays and caving and climbing training courses are organised by the Dales Centre which is also based in Grassington. There are two car parks in Grassington. The largest is near the Information Centre off the Pateley Bridge, B6265, road.

A Ghaistrill's Strid. An attractive picnic site next to a narrow river channel of strangely carved limestone rocks. Do not attempt to jump the Strid (Stride): the Wharfe flows deep and fast.

B Grass Wood Nature Reserve is owned and maintained by the Yorkshire Naturalists Trust. Visitors are allowed to use the right of way through the wood but are expected to observe a few simple rules and respect the wildlife of this unique woodland habitat. Many varieties of spring flowers, including lily of the valley and much rarer plants, bloom in Grass Wood. Please do not pick any of them as it often kills the parent plant.

C Viewpoint. Dramatic Kilnsey Crag can be seen about 1¼ miles (2 km) to the north-west, upstream, of this point. The crag is a popular climbing area for rock gymnasts but the less energetic can enjoy the amenities of the Kilnsey Trout Farm and nearby angling pools.

D Viewpoint. Trees have overgrown the ancient settlement but many of its substantial walls can still be traced. Here is an old village which predates Georgian Grassington and was built across what was once an open treeless hillside. The Black Death wiped out most of its inhabitants and the farms and houses were abandoned to nature. Beautiful Grass Wood now covers a scene of sickness and tragedy.

over

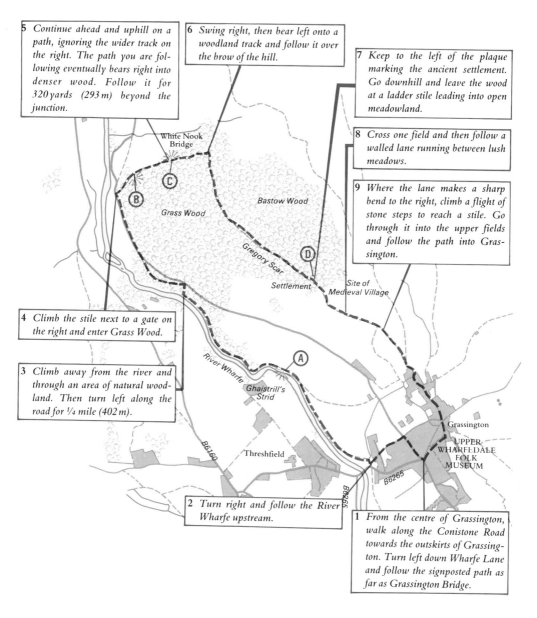

5 *Continue ahead and uphill on a path, ignoring the wider track on the right. The path you are following eventually bears right into denser wood. Follow it for 320 yards (293 m) beyond the junction.*

6 *Swing right, then bear left onto a woodland track and follow it over the brow of the hill.*

7 *Keep to the left of the plaque marking the ancient settlement. Go downhill and leave the wood at a ladder stile leading into open meadowland.*

8 *Cross one field and then follow a walled lane running between lush meadows.*

9 *Where the lane makes a sharp bend to the right, climb a flight of stone steps to reach a stile. Go through it into the upper fields and follow the path into Grassington.*

White Nook
Bridge

Bastow Wood

Grass Wood

Gregory Scar

Settlement

Site of
Medieval Village

4 *Climb the stile next to a gate on the right and enter Grass Wood.*

3 *Climb away from the river and through an area of natural woodland. Then turn left along the road for ¼ mile (402 m).*

River Wharfe

Ghaistrill's
Strid

Grassington

UPPER
WHARFEDALE
FOLK
MUSEUM

B6160

Threshfield

B6265

B6265

2 *Turn right and follow the River Wharfe upstream.*

1 *From the centre of Grassington, walk along the Conistone Road towards the outskirts of Grassington. Turn left down Wharfe Lane and follow the signposted path as far as Grassington Bridge.*

Walk 23

MALHAM COVE AND GORDALE SCAR

4¾ miles (7.6 km) Moderate/strenuous; one climb of 377 feet (115 m)

Most of the thousands of visitors who come to Malham each year do so by following the delightful scenic road which leaves the A65 at Gargrave. The village can get crowded but its fame is justified and the National Park Authority, by careful planning control, has enabled it to retain much of its charm. This walk avoids the more popular routes and uses lesser-known paths to reach the spectacular rock formations of Malham Cove and neighbouring Gordale Scar.

A Malham. A typical Dales' village, it has shops, two pubs and several cafés. The bridge was originally built for pack horses but has been widened to cope with modern traffic.

B Malham Cove. The stream issuing from the foot of the overhanging limestone crag inspired Charles Kingsley to write his 'Water Babies' novel. Despite appearances to the contrary, this is not the infant River Aire but a stream which has travelled beneath the moors well to the north-west of Malham. The Aire begins its life as Malham Tarn and then disappears underground at Water Sinks, south of the tarn, before resurfacing at Aire Head Springs beyond the village. The main river is, therefore, beneath the stream which appears at the foot of the Cove. Malham Tarn is a unique feature in the normally dry limestone landscape. It owes its occurrence to a layer of impervious rock below the natural depression now filled by the lake. The river has not always been underground. Until the 1700's, a waterfall higher than Niagara cascaded over the 300 foot (91 m) high cliff of Malham Cove, which overhangs some 20 feet (6 m).

C The bare limestone pavement is fissured by deep north/south-aligned 'grikes'. Plants growing in their shady recesses, such as hart's tongue fern and dog's mercury, are associated with the ground cover of an ash wood, which covered most of the fells before the last Ice Age.

D Viewpoint. Upper Airedale stretches towards the hazy line of western hills which mark its widest limits. Beyond Gargrave is the Aire – Calder gap. This is a natural break in the Pennines and it has provided a low-level, all-weather route for travellers since prehistoric times.

The fields directly below Malham Cove still show the outlines of their medieval pattern.

E The dry valley on the left is the ancient course of the River Aire before its disappearance underground. A well-made drystone wall follows the dale and marks the boundary between lands belonging to Fountains and Bolton Abbeys. Much of the wealth of these abbeys grew, in medieval times, from lead mining and the extensive sheep walks (grazings) which covered the land hereabouts.

F There is a cathedral-like atmosphere beneath the towering cliffs of Gordale Scar. The gorge is a collapsed cave system carved by melt water at the end of the last Ice Age. A waterfall now cascades down a cliff composed of tufa, reformed deposits of limestone on moss. The stream flows out of a 'window' in rocks above the fall. It is possible to reach the top of the waterfall and continue the walk out onto Malham Lings moor but it involves a wet and often slippery rock climb up the face of the tufa outcrop. It is safer, therefore, to follow the route as described and return from this point. On the way back from Gordale you can look for water-cress in the stream-bed.

G Janet's Foss. The waterfall is created by moss 'fossilised' by tufa deposits which have built up into an attractive green outcrop.

Janet is a friendly fairy who lives in the hollow beside the foss. 'Foss' is a Dales' word for waterfall and comes from the Old Norse.

H Wild garlic, bluebells, wood anemones, dog's mercury and violets grow in the shade of the ash woodland.

over

0   1 mile

0   1 km

4 *Follow the limestone pavement to the right, keeping well back from the edge, especially in wet or windy weather. Climb a ladder stile and bear right uphill on a waymarked grassy path.*

5 *Cross ladder stiles on both sides of the road and follow the grassy path downhill.*

6 *Turn left at Gordale Bridge. Follow the signposted streamside path as far as the waterfall and return to this point.*

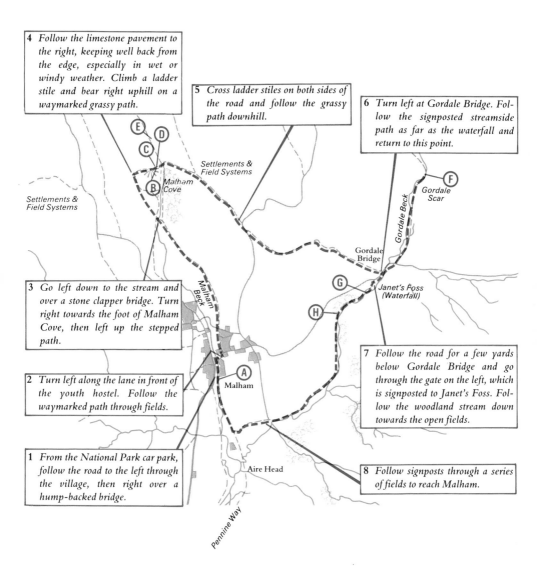

Settlements & Field Systems

Settlements & Field Systems

Malham Cove

Gordale Scar

Gordale Beck

Gordale Bridge

Malham Beck

Janet's Foss (Waterfall)

3 *Go left down to the stream and over a stone clapper bridge. Turn right towards the foot of Malham Cove, then left up the stepped path.*

Malham

2 *Turn left along the lane in front of the youth hostel. Follow the waymarked path through fields.*

7 *Follow the road for a few yards below Gordale Bridge and go through the gate on the left, which is signposted to Janet's Foss. Follow the woodland stream down towards the open fields.*

1 *From the National Park car park, follow the road to the left through the village, then right over a hump-backed bridge.*

Aire Head

8 *Follow signposts through a series of fields to reach Malham.*

Pennine Way

Walk 24
GRIMWITH RESERVOIR
6¼ miles (10 km) Easy

The name belies the attraction of this recently extended reservoir which is about 4 miles (6.4 km) east of Grassington and ¾ mile (1.2 km) to the north of the B6265 road. The walk takes advantage of specially created concessionary footpaths around the reservoir and access is either from the dam side car park or by a moorland path from a lay-by at the side of the B6265.

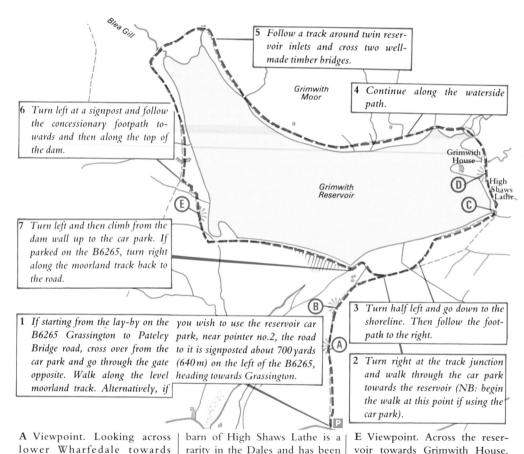

Blea Gill

5 *Follow a track around twin reservoir inlets and cross two well-made timber bridges.*

Grimwith Moor

4 *Continue along the waterside path.*

6 *Turn left at a signpost and follow the concessionary footpath towards and then along the top of the dam.*

Grimwith House

Grimwith Reservoir

D

High Shaws Lathe

E

C

7 *Turn left and then climb from the dam wall up to the car park. If parked on the B6265, turn right along the moorland track back to the road.*

B

A

3 *Turn half left and go down to the shoreline. Then follow the footpath to the right.*

1 *If starting from the lay-by on the B6265 Grassington to Pateley Bridge road, cross over from the car park and go through the gate opposite. Walk along the level moorland track. Alternatively, if you wish to use the reservoir car park, near pointer no.2, the road to it is signposted about 700 yards (640 m) on the left of the B6265, heading towards Grassington.*

2 *Turn right at the track junction and walk through the car park towards the reservoir (NB: begin the walk at this point if using the car park).*

P

A Viewpoint. Looking across lower Wharfedale towards heather-clad Burnsall Moor.

B Viewpoint of the reservoir in its moorland setting.

C The heather-thatched cruck-barn of High Shaws Lathe is a rarity in the Dales and has been renovated as part of the amenity development of the reservoir.

D Viewpoint. Abandoned Grimwith House, to your left, sits attractively on a low promontory.

E Viewpoint. Across the reservoir towards Grimwith House. Waterfowl, such as Canada Geese, are now breeding around this secluded man-made moorland water.

Walk 25
CRACOE FELL
6 miles (9.7 km) Strenuous; one climb of 922 feet (281 m)

```
0                        1 mile
├────┴────┴────┴────┴────┤
0            1 km
```

Cracoe Fell is part of the Duke of Devonshire's Chatsworth Estate. Free access is allowed at all times other than days when grouse shooting takes place, or during periods of drought or high fire risk. Check beforehand with the estate office (Bolton Abbey 227), or the National Park Information Centre (Grassington 752748).

The moorland walk is from the village of Cracoe, which is about 3¼ miles (5.2 km) southwest of Grassington along the B6265 Skipton road. The Devonshire Arms in the centre of the village will provide refreshment after the walk. Roadside parking can usually be found around the village.

1 From the Skipton end of Cracoe, turn left, then left again along a narrow winding lane.

2 Turn right at the 'T' junction and follow the walled track towards the open fell.

3 Bear left away from a sheep pen at the track end. Then zig-zag steadily uphill on the pathless moor. Aim a little to the left of the prominent skyline pinnacle.

8 Turn right at the narrow gate opposite Rylstone church. Follow the path across one field, through another gate and along a leafy lane back to Cracoe.

4 Bear left, then right along the rocky moorland crest and climb up to rocks surrounding a stone pinnacle.

7 Turn right at the track junction and then over a stile to follow a field path signposted to Cracoe.

6 Go through a gap in the wall on the right, then downhill on a recessed track marked by blue-topped stakes.

5 Climb the ladder stile opposite the pinnacle. Bear right to follow the gently descending moorland boundary wall.

(Map labels: Cracoe, Fell Lane (Track), Chapel Lane (Track), Fish Ponds, War Memorial Obelisk, Manor House, Rylstone, Hall Fell, Rylstone Fell, Cross, A, B, C, D, E, F)

A Cracoe's water supply comes from the fenced off Three Thorn Well.

B Viewpoint. The pinnacle commemorates the local dead of the First World War. It looks out over Wharfedale on your right and Airedale and Craven to the left.

C The wind-worn rocks are composed of gritstone. Heather and bilberry grow on the nearby grouse moor.

D A stone at the side of the path marked with the letters C & R is the boundary of Cracoe and Rylstone parishes.

E The prominent cross on the right is centuries old.

F Depressions on the right are the remains of medieval fish-ponds and were probably part of nearby monastic buildings which have since disappeared. The Norton family, squires of Rylstone, who died for the Catholic cause in the 'Rising of the North' of 1569, lived at nearby Rylstone Manor (across the fields on your left). Francis Norton was immortalised by William Wordsworth in his 'White Doe of Rylstone', the moving poem which tells the story of the white doe Norton gave to his sister, Emily. She used to take it with her when she visited his grave in Bolton Abbey, moving 'like a gliding ghost' along the path which you have followed down from the moors.

43

Walk 26
BOLTON ABBEY AND STRID WOOD
6¼ miles (10 km) Easy/moderate

Bolton Abbey is a renowned beauty spot with good road access. The A59 links it to both North Yorkshire and Lancashire and the B6160 leaves the A65 at Addingham, a direct route from West Yorkshire. There are car parks both in Bolton Abbey village and near the Cavendish Pavilion (pointer no.3).

North of Bolton Abbey, Strid Wood is privately owned as part of the Duke of Devonshire's Chatsworth Estate. The public are allowed to use footpaths on both sides of the river but a small toll must be paid for the privilege, the money being used for the upkeep of the woods and for the maintenance of a nature trail.

Bolton Abbey village is owned by the Chatsworth Estate Trust and a number of its workers live in attractive cottages surrounding the village. An ancient tythe barn in the village is now a café and the Devonshire Arms, closer to the junction with the A59, is a very comfortable and hospitable inn.

A The narrow triple archway over the road once carried an aqueduct supplying water to the priory mill, which is now used as a holiday cottage.

B Viewpoint. This is the first of the many and ever-changing views of Bolton Abbey. The title 'abbey' is, in fact, a misnomer and it should correctly be termed 'priory', a small religious house separate from the main ecclesiastical foundation which belonged to the Augustinian Black Canons. They founded their priory first in 1120 in nearby Embsay and moved to this flat riverside site given to them by Alizia de Romilly, lady of Skipton Castle, and her son, William, in 1154. The order prospered on this spot for 385 years, controlling interests in lead mining and sheep farming.

The curving river and majestic ruins have inspired many artists such as Turner, Girtin and Cox, as well as gifted amateurs of the present time.

C Cavendish Memorial. The ornate six-sided fountain was built in memory of Lord Frederick Cavendish, who was assassinated in Phoenix Park, Dublin, in 1882.

D Cavendish Pavilion. Originally used by visiting sportsmen, the well-preserved Edwardian pavilion now serves refreshments.

E Strid Wood. The well-maintained woodland is home to a wide range of birdlife and small animals. Woodland flowers, such as bluebells and anemones, flourish in spring in the semi-shaded conditions provided by the trees before they come into leaf.

F The Strid. This narrow and dangerous cleft is carved by the Wharfe cutting its way through a band of soft limestone. The torrent roars its way through the chasm, a trap for many unwary or foolhardy people, who have tried to jump or 'strid' across the deceptive gap. Legend has it that Boy of Egremont, the son of Alizia de Romilly, was one of its victims. Another story tells that a white horse appears shortly before anyone is about to be drowned in the Strid – so beware if you see one!

The Strid is at its best when the river is high but if you want to see the curiously worn rocks of its sides, then wait until we have had several weeks of drought.

G The substantially built stone 'bridge' is really an aqueduct carrying water from Bradford Corporation's Nidderdale reservoirs towards the West Riding.

Look upstream beyond the parapet and you will get a glimpse of Barden Tower, a ruined hunting lodge which was once the property of the powerful Clifford family of whom Lady Anne, indefatigable 17th-century Dales traveller, is best remembered. Barden Tower is one of the finest old buildings in the Dales. The ruins are open to the public and art courses are held in the attached studio.

H The downstream path is arguably more attractive than that on the opposite bank. The valley sides are steeper and the river
over

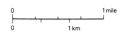

views are edged by gnarled oaks and stately beech trees. Bird life is more active on this less frequented side.

The main path keeps a fairly level course and side paths usually rejoin it after wandering up or down towards some interesting feature.

I Viewpoint. Bolton Priory stands above a wide sweep of the River Wharfe.

J Bolton Priory. The Augustinian Black Canons who lived here each wore a black cassock and a sleeved surplice with a hooded cloak fastened only at the neck. They wore a black square cap. Even though the order was prosperous, the monks were sworn to a life of poverty, obedience and chastity. They prayed seven times daily and spent the rest of their day looking after the needs of local people. Life, however, was not always tranquil: in both 1318 and 1320 Black Douglas, the Scottish raider, attacked Bolton Abbey during his deadly forays into Craven.

Richard Moon was the last prior. He tried to save Bolton Abbey from dissolution by a bribe of £10 sent to Thomas Cromwell, Henry VIII's lieutenant, but this had no effect and the monks were driven out into the world on 29th January 1540. The abbey soon fell into ruin, its stones used in local buildings, but the nave was saved and became the parish church.

K On your way up to the 'hole in the wall', look out for wide depressions on either side of the path. These were fish ponds supplying carp to the priory.

5 Go over a wooden bridge across a side stream and then out into an open field.

6 Turn right across the stone bridge and then right again on its far side. Walk downstream on a grassy path and into predominantly oak and beech wood.

7 Cross the wooden stile and turn right, downhill along the road for about 130 yards (119 m). Go over the road bridge and turn right along the woodland path signposted to Cavendish and Bolton Abbey.

4 Continue along the rocky woodland path, upstream at first, following purple, then yellow waymarks.

8 Continue downstream beyond the wooden bridge (the Pavilion is opposite if you are in need of refreshment).

3 Do not cross the river by the wooden bridge but follow the woodland path beyond the pavilion. Follow green markers beyond the toll gate.

9 Climb up to the road. Follow it, over the ford, then right at a footpath sign to Bolton Priory.

2 Bear right at the memorial, over a stile and down a flight of wooden steps to your left. Walk upstream, through the riverside meadows at Sand Holme.

1 Follow the road through Bolton Abbey village as far as the Cavendish Memorial.

10 Cross the footbridge, or the Friar's Steps if the river is low enough. Follow the path to the left of the abbey and climb up to a hole in the high boundary wall. The village is along the road to your left.

Walk 27
SIMON'S SEAT

4 miles (6.4 km) Strenuous; one climb of 1122 feet (342 m)

The best approach is by way of Appletreewick, which is off the B6160. Drive down the Barden Bridge road for ½ mile (0.8 km). Park beyond the bridge below Howgill chapel.

Appletreewick — the locals pronounce it 'Ap'trick' — has two pubs and both supply meals.

Several old houses, at least 400 years old, indicate the age of this village. It was once classed as a township, being granted a charter in 1311 to hold an annual Onion Fair.

Simon's Seat, the high point of this walk, is on Barden Fell grouse moor. Although access is free for most of the year, there will be days when the moor is closed for shooting, or during drought and periods of high fire risk. Check locally with the Chatsworth Estate Office (Bolton Abbey 227) or the Yorkshire Dales National Park Information Centre (Grassington 752748).

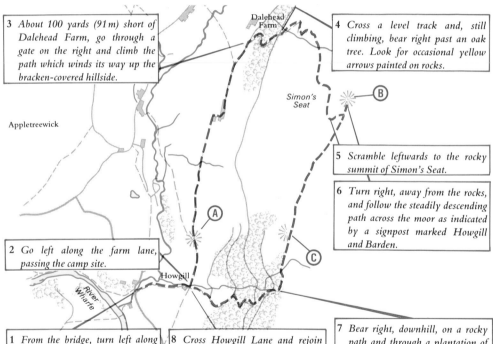

3 *About 100 yards (91 m) short of Dalehead Farm, go through a gate on the right and climb the path which winds its way up the bracken-covered hillside.*

4 *Cross a level track and, still climbing, bear right past an oak tree. Look for occasional yellow arrows painted on rocks.*

Dalehead Farm

Simon's Seat

Ⓑ

Appletreewick

5 *Scramble leftwards to the rocky summit of Simon's Seat.*

6 *Turn right, away from the rocks, and follow the steadily descending path across the moor as indicated by a signpost marked Howgill and Barden.*

Ⓐ

Ⓒ

2 *Go left along the farm lane, passing the camp site.*

Howgill

River Wharfe

7 *Bear right, downhill, on a rocky path and through a plantation of pine trees.*

1 *From the bridge, turn left along the sandy lane into Howgill.*

8 *Cross Howgill Lane and rejoin the track down to the road bridge.*

A Viewpoint. Barden's woodlands cloak Lower Wharfedale with Barden Moor as their backcloth. Fir Beck joins the main dale directly below the viewpoint. Parcevall Hall, with its attractive gardens (open to the public on advertised days), is upstream of Fir Beck and beyond the hall is Trollers Gill, a narrow ravine with an eerie echo.

B Viewpoint. The view makes the climb worthwhile. Wharfe-dale cuts a deep winding trough to the north and the broad spread of Ilkley Moor is to the south.

C Viewpoint of the hamlet and farmsteads of Howgill sheltering below a tree-covered hillock.

Walk 28
ATTERMIRE SCAR

5 miles (8 km) Moderate/strenuous; total climb of 700 feet (213 m)

The walk starts from the centre of Settle, 'capital' of Upper Ribblesdale. This is a busy market town on the A65 and there are parking facilities near the market place. Settle is also the southern terminus of the scenic Settle to Carlisle railway. Soon after leaving the bustle of the town, steep but easy-to-follow paths climb to the limestone wilderness of Attermire Scar. Several small caves penetrate its craggy lower slopes. A torch is desirable if you plan to explore their depths. The return is by a gently descending field track with wide-ranging views of Ribblesdale and the Craven district.

6 *At the point where the track joins the road, turn left through a small gate and follow a field path along the bottom edge of a mature wood.*

5 *Turn left through a metal gate and follow the well-made farm track downhill.*

7 *Use the gate in the narrow gap between two sections of woodland.*

8 *Take the stile at the side of the wicket gate. Walk ahead along a field path and descend by an improving track into the outskirts of Settle.*

2 *Bear right, away from the road and follow the rough-walled lane uphill.*

3 *About 100 yards (91 m) beyond a clump of trees, turn right at a signpost to Malham. Climb the grassy hillside. At first, there is no path but one soon develops. Follow this to the right of the boundary wall.*

4 *Cross two stiles and then go through a gap in the wall. Turn left and climb the rocky path along the foot of the crags.*

1 *Follow the road to the left of the market place and climb towards Constitution Hill.*

Langcliffe

Jubilee Cave

Victoria Cave

Ⓒ

Brent Scar

Attermire Scar

Warrendale Knotts

Ⓐ

Ⓑ

Caves

Horseshoe Cave

Settle

A Viewpoint across the townscape of Settle and the Ribble Valley with the Ingleborough fells on the right.

B Viewpoint. The limestone crags of Attermire Scar, the surface indication of the line of a major geological fault, fill the steep hillside on your left giving it the appearance of a much higher mountain. Malham Moor is directly ahead.

C The caves of Attermire Scar. Attermire Cave is above direction pointer 4 and four small caves surround Victoria Cave near the highest point of the climb. Jubilee Cave, so named because of its discovery at the time of Queen Victoria's Jubilee, is about 110 yards (101 m) uphill beyond pointer no.5. Traces of habitation from pre-historic to post-Roman times have been found in some of the caves.

CATRIGG FORCE AND STAINFORTH FORCE

5 miles (8 km) Moderate

0   ¼ mile

0   ½ km

From the car park beside the B6479, the route is through the quiet village of Stainforth to reach the first waterfall, or 'force'. Easy field paths and then a fairly steep woodland track lead down to the unspoilt village of Langcliffe built around its spacious green. A pleasant riverside stroll follows the Ribble upstream to the second force.

1 *Walk through Stainforth and turn left along the lane opposite the Craven Heifer Inn.*

Catrigg Force (Waterfall)

(A) (B)

Upper Winskill

Stainforth

Lower Winskill

11 *Turn right at the bridge. Follow the narrow lane up to the main road. Stainforth is on the right.*

(C)

(D)

River Ribble

Stainforth Force (Waterfall)

Langcliffe

10 *Cross the river by a footbridge and turn right, upstream. Follow the river-bank, using stiles and gaps in boundary walls.*

9 *Cross the bridge and take the lane on the left, down to a group of riverside cottages.*

2 *Turn right in front of a group of cottages on the far side of a tiny green. Follow the walled lane marked 'Unsuitable for Motors'.*

3 *Climb the stile next to the lane-head gate. Turn right and cross the open field.*

4 *Climb the stile and bear right as directed by the signpost towards Winskill Farm.*

5 *Do not go into the farm-yard but keep ahead through a gate and then downhill along the track signposted to Langcliffe.*

6 *Climb a ladder stile on the left. Walk downhill through a series of rocky fields.*

7 *Follow a narrow rocky path down-hill through a narrow belt of gnarled trees. Go through a small gate and continue downhill, above and to the left of an old quarry. Cross three fields to reach the access lane into Langcliffe.*

8 *Bear right at the village green and walk down to the main road. Turn right again to the railway bridge.*

A The short signposted downhill path on the left leads to the deep wooded cleft of Catrigg Force. Force is a Dales' dialect word for waterfall and comes from the Norse 'foss'.

B Viewpoint. Ingleborough's stepped slopes are to the left, then Penyghent and finally the sprawling bulk of Fountains Fell on the right.

C Viewpoint. The western hills of Craven mark the far horizon across the deep trough of the Ribble Valley.

D Viewpoint. Stainforth Force is backed by the graceful arch of an old packhorse bridge, part of a centuries-old road between Lan-caster and York.

FEIZOR

4¼ miles (6.8 km) Easy

Riverside parking for the start of this walk is usually available at the Little Stainforth camp-site; otherwise park beside the B6479 in Stainforth and follow the side lane for about ½ mile (0.8 km) to Little Stainforth. A little-used path beyond the camp-site crosses a grassy moor to reach Feizor (pronounced Fayzr). The return is by way of Feizor Thwaite.

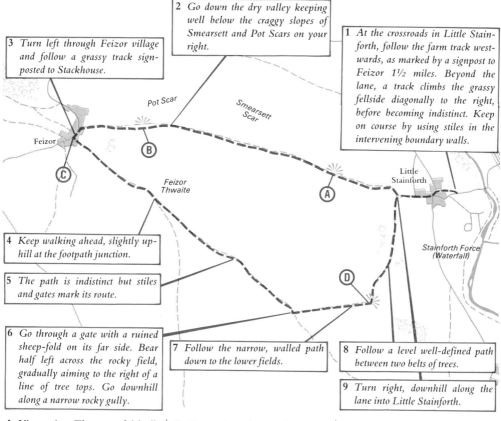

2 *Go down the dry valley keeping well below the craggy slopes of Smearsett and Pot Scars on your right.*

3 *Turn left through Feizor village and follow a grassy track signposted to Stackhouse.*

1 *At the crossroads in Little Stainforth, follow the farm track westwards, as marked by a signpost to Feizor 1½ miles. Beyond the lane, a track climbs the grassy fellside diagonally to the right, before becoming indistinct. Keep on course by using stiles in the intervening boundary walls.*

Pot Scar

Smearsett Scar

Feizor

Feizor Thwaite

Little Stainforth

Stainforth Force (Waterfall)

4 *Keep walking ahead, slightly uphill at the footpath junction.*

5 *The path is indistinct but stiles and gates mark its route.*

6 *Go through a gate with a ruined sheep-fold on its far side. Bear half left across the rocky field, gradually aiming to the right of a line of tree tops. Go downhill along a narrow rocky gully.*

7 *Follow the narrow, walled path down to the lower fields.*

8 *Follow a level well-defined path between two belts of trees.*

9 *Turn right, downhill along the lane into Little Stainforth.*

A Viewpoint. The graceful bulk of Penyghent, about 4 miles (6.4 m) away on the left of the skyline, contrasts with the long whaleback of Fountains Fell. Both are crossed by the Pennine Way.

B Viewpoint. The Bowland Fells are away to the left and, on a clear day, Morecambe Bay glints in the distance far beyond the Lune Valley.

C Feizor. This remote hill-farming village is well away from the disturbing effect of busy roads. A few modern houses fill the gaps between traditional Dales' cottages and farmhouses.

D Viewpoint. Penyghent appears suddenly through a gap in the hillside.

Walk 31
PENYGHENT
6 miles (9.7 km) Strenuous, muddy sections; one climb of 1522 ft (464 m)

Penyghent is one of the few real peaks in the Pennines. Most of the other summits are simply the highest points in an area of wild moorland. Here we have one of the most graceful English mountains; its slopes benignly dominate Horton in Ribblesdale, a busy village on the B6479 and the starting place for this ascent of Penyghent. Horton is also the usual start and finishing point for the gruelling race, or individual attempts, on the 'Three Peaks', of which Penyghent is one. The other two are Whernside, above the graceful span of Ribblehead

Viaduct north-west of Horton, and Ingelborough, to the south of Whernside and closer to Horton. The distance involved is about 24 miles (38.6 km) and has been completed in under four hours by fell runners but ordinary walkers need over 12 hours of daylight for safety.

Penyghent's stepped outline follows the sharply defined changes of its geological structure. The flat summit is surrounded by crags and boulder fields made of millstone grit, the sediment of an ancient river delta; below it and older in descend-

ing order come, at first, layers of shales and sandstones, again the debris of the prehistoric delta. Then at the foot of the mountain, and covering the nearby moorland, are carboniferous limestones formed in a tropical sea. Vertical crags and detached pinnacles feature on the steepest part of the mountain while, lower down, the relatively flat moor is dotted with pot holes and sinks where streams disappear. They reappear in the valley bottom closer to the village, which sits on a layer of impervious silurian slate.

A Horton church. A typical Dales' church; its roof is made from locally mined lead and the flags of its floor are made of slate taken from nearby quarries; the doorway is Norman but the beautiful stained glass window in its south wall is modern. Pillars dividing the nave slope to the south – a curious traditional feature of the area.

B A wooden walkway is helping prevent further erosion on boggy stretches of the climb.

C Viewpoint. Whernside and Ingleborough are across the Ribble Valley. Fountains Fell, to the south-east, is crossed by the Pennine Way path, which has climbed Penyghent from Dale Head to the south of Fawcett Moor, before descending to Horton.

The various strata or bands of rock which make Penyghent's distinctive shape are clearly defined on the climb from Brackenbottom. Limestone gives way, in turn, to sandstone, shales and eventually, millstone grit on the summit. All the rocks were laid down in a tropical sea which became inundated by a muddy river delta.

D Notice the detached limestone pinnacle beyond the footpath junction. Alpine purple saxifrage hangs from the limestone crags in April and early May.

E Hunt Pot. This deep pothole is a few yards to the left of the path. Take great care as the rock around its lip is very slippery. Water flowing into the dark depths of Hunt Pot reappears as Brants Gill, near the Crown

Hotel. Douk Ghyll, the stream which you followed from Horton Church, flows from Hull Pot to the north-west of Hunt Pot, the two streams managing to cross each other underground.

F The lane is one of the ancient green roads of the Pennines. This one was a packhorse way, linking Ribblesdale and Littondale.

G Ever-changing views of Penyghent standing proudly above its dramatic limestone moors, can be enjoyed almost all the way down to Horton in Ribblesdale.

H Viewpoint. Ingleborough is opposite, marred only by the ugly intrusion of Horton Quarry, reminding us of the price we must pay for good road surfaces and high-quality steel.
over

50

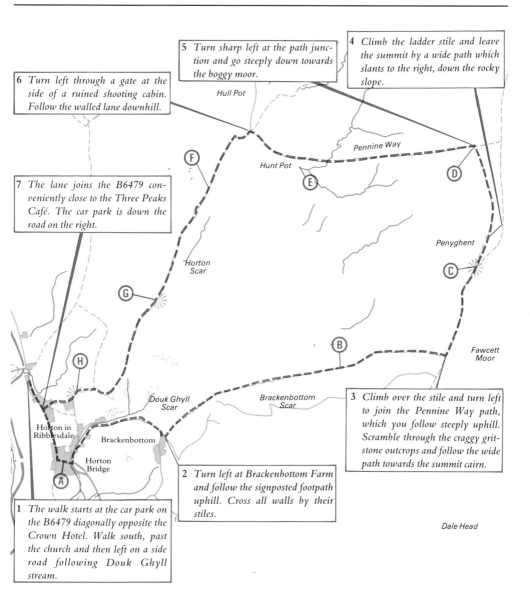

5 Turn sharp left at the path junction and go steeply down towards the boggy moor.

4 Climb the ladder stile and leave the summit by a wide path which slants to the right, down the rocky slope.

6 Turn left through a gate at the side of a ruined shooting cabin. Follow the walled lane downhill.

7 The lane joins the B6479 conveniently close to the Three Peaks Café. The car park is down the road on the right.

3 Climb over the stile and turn left to join the Pennine Way path, which you follow steeply uphill. Scramble through the craggy gritstone outcrops and follow the wide path towards the summit cairn.

2 Turn left at Brackenbottom Farm and follow the signposted footpath uphill. Cross all walls by their stiles.

1 The walk starts at the car park on the B6479 diagonally opposite the Crown Hotel. Walk south, past the church and then left on a side road following Douk Ghyll stream.

Hull Pot

Pennine Way

Hunt Pot

Penyghent

Horton Scar

Fawcett Moor

Douk Ghyll Scar

Brackenbottom Scar

Horton in Ribblesdale

Brackenbottom

Horton Bridge

Dale Head

Walk 32
HORTON IN RIBBLESDALE
5 miles (8km) Easy

This walk follows the Ribble from Horton in Ribblesdale, a popular village on the B6479 Settle to Ribblehead road. A riverside stroll is followed by a gentle uphill ramble through fields which, in turn, leads to quiet byways surrounding Horton.

1 *From the car park in Horton in Ribblesdale, cross the footbridge and turn left on a field path, away from the road. Follow the riverbank downstream.*

2 *Avoid a wide bend in the river by turning right as directed by a signpost. Cross the field and join a sunken lane.*

3 *Cross the river by the footbridge and bear left over the fields using stiles in their walls. Turn left along the road.*

4 *Turn right and follow the side road as far as a barn near the next junction with the main road. Follow the signpost on the right to Dub Cote. There is no path but keep to the right of a second barn and then left over the stile.*

5 *Climb two adjacent fields, crossing a ladder stile over their boundary wall. Keep to the left of White Sike Barn and then turn right along a walled track.*

8 *Turn left at the lane junction, downhill into Horton. The main car park is to the right along the road.*

7 *Turn right, cross the stream by a footbridge and then turn right again. Follow the lane signposted 'Pennine Way'.*

6 *Go to the right along the road, uphill past Brackenbottom Farm and then downhill by the side of Douk Ghyll.*

Horton in Ribblesdale

River Ribble

Brackenbottom

Horton Bridge

Dub Cote

C

B

White Sike Barn

A

Studfold

A Viewpoint. A log bridge spanning the Ribble makes an interesting foreground to the view of Penyghent. The river is an excellent trout stream where visiting and resident birds take advantage of the unspoilt environment of its quiet banks.

B Viewpoint. You can see Horton and the Upper Ribble Valley with the eastern slopes of Ingleborough to the far left.

C Dub Cote Bunk House. This is one of several redundant barns throughout the Yorkshire Dales, which have been converted into simple accommodation. For further details, tel: Horton in Ribblesdale 238.

Walk 33
UPPER LITTONDALE
4 miles (6.4 km) Moderate

Wild Upper Littondale is one of the least visited places in the Dales. A tributary of Wharfedale, its stark moorland solitude contrasts with more popular areas. The valley road leaves the B6160 at Skirfare Bridge between Kettlewell and Kilnsey and makes a sharp left turn at Halton Gill to climb beneath Penyghent on its way to Stainforth. A short cul-de-sac road from Halton Gill continues for about a mile to Foxup and it is from here that the walk starts. Roadside parking is limited but a few spaces can usually be found near Foxup Bridge.

6 Cross the road to the left of Halton Gill Bridge. Continue by riverside field path back to Foxup Bridge.

1 Turn left opposite Foxup Bridge Farm and go through a gate. Climb the grassy track signposted to Horton in Ribblesdale.

2 Bear left, away from the wall as indicated by a signpost. There is no clear path but the route is marked by blue-topped posts.

3 Turn right along the metalled road and follow it for about ⅓ of a mile (536 m).

4 Turn sharp left at a signpost and follow a wire fence diagonally downhill to Nether Heselden Farm.

5 Go through the farm-yard and turn left, then go through a gate at the side of a large circular slurry tank. Follow the signposted route across a series of fields.

Foxup
Foxup Beck
Halton Gill
Halton Gill Bridge
Berghle (Pot Hole)
Calena Pot
Red Dot Pots
Flamethrower Hole
Littondale
River Skirfare
Settlement & Field System
Hesleden
Penyghent Gill

A Notice how the sturdy farmhouses at Foxup turn their backs to the cold north wind.

B Viewpoint. Looking down Littondale towards Wharfedale in the hazy distance.

C Viewpoint. Penyghent can be seen ahead with Fountains Fell on the left.

D Viewpoint. The deep ravine of Penyghent Gill is on the right. The trees along the river-bank are remnants of forests which covered the Dales before the last Ice Age.

Walk 34
THE KNIGHTS' TEMPLAR CHAPEL
4 miles (6.4 km) Easy

Knights' Templars were members of a mystical semi-military religious order which was founded by Crusaders in Jerusalem in 1118 but was suppressed in 1312. The poignant ruins of one of their chapels is the turning point of this pleasant rural stroll. From West Witton, 4 miles (6.4 km) east of Aysgarth along the A684, the way is first along an easy high-level grassy terrace and the return by way of quiet meadows between Swinithwaite and the River Ure. Park near the start of the walk at West Witton, away from the main road and, if possible, away from any houses.

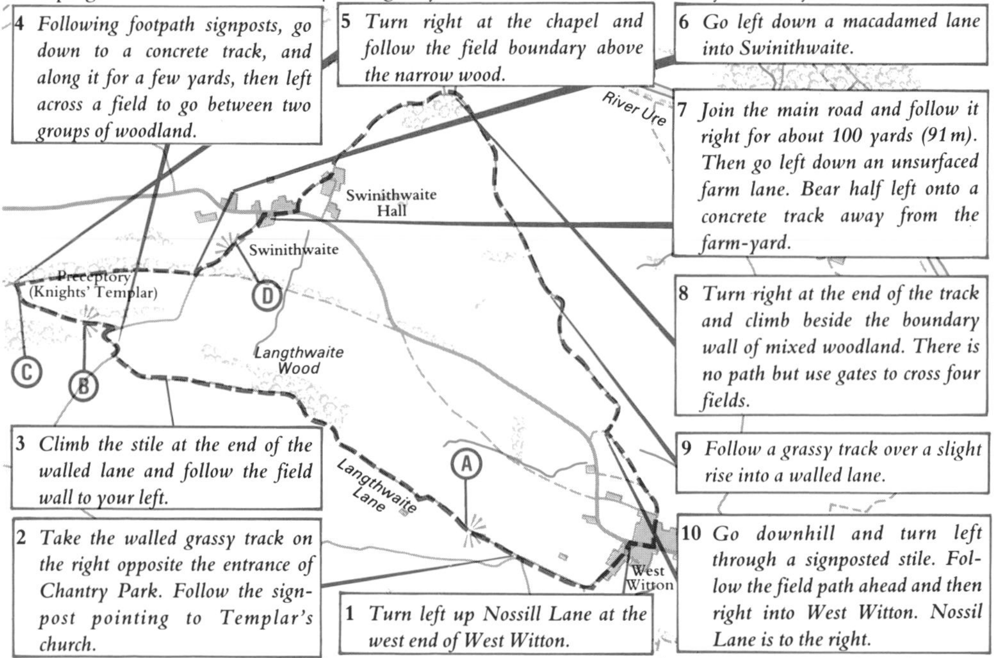

4 *Following footpath signposts, go down to a concrete track, and along it for a few yards, then left across a field to go between two groups of woodland.*

5 *Turn right at the chapel and follow the field boundary above the narrow wood.*

6 *Go left down a macadamed lane into Swinithwaite.*

7 *Join the main road and follow it right for about 100 yards (91 m). Then go left down an unsurfaced farm lane. Bear half left onto a concrete track away from the farm-yard.*

8 *Turn right at the end of the track and climb beside the boundary wall of mixed woodland. There is no path but use gates to cross four fields.*

3 *Climb the stile at the end of the walled lane and follow the field wall to your left.*

9 *Follow a grassy track over a slight rise into a walled lane.*

2 *Take the walled grassy track on the right opposite the entrance of Chantry Park. Follow the signpost pointing to Templar's church.*

10 *Go downhill and turn left through a signposted stile. Follow the field path ahead and then right into West Witton. Nossil Lane is to the right.*

1 *Turn left up Nossill Lane at the west end of West Witton.*

Map labels: River Ure, Swinithwaite Hall, Swinithwaite, Preceptory (Knights' Templar), D, C, B, A, Langthwaite Wood, Langthwaite Lane, West Witton

A Viewpoint. West Witton is below in the pastoral lower reaches of Wensleydale. The village is old enough to be mentioned in the Domesday Book where it is referred to as both Witun and Witone. The name is Old English for 'the farm by the wood'. Traces of the forest which once filled Wensleydale can be seen on the nearby stepped hillside.

They burn an effigy of 'Owd Bartle' in West Witton for St. Bartholomew's day on the nearest Saturday to 24th August.

B Viewpoint. Wensleydale is framed by the edges of twin woodlands lining the steep hillside.

C The Templar Chapel or Preceptory. The outline of the tiny chapel and a few stone coffins are the scant surface remains of this mystical order which vanished long ago.

D Viewpoint. Castle Bolton can be seen on the opposite hillside. Mary, Queen of Scots was held prisoner there from July 1567 to January 1569 on her slow journey south to her eventual execution. The castle was held in the name of the Crown during the Civil War but its defenders were starved into submission by Cromwell's troops in 1645.

Walk 35
CENTRAL SWALEDALE
3¾ miles (6 km) Easy; one climb of 354 feet (108 m)

An attraction before or after the walk is the Punch Bowl Inn at Feetham. The route of the walk is an irregular oval centred upon this hospitable pub. Feetham is roughly 3¾ miles (6 km) west of Reeth along the B6270 in central Swaledale. As parking near the start of the walk is limited, it will probably be better to leave the car in Feetham.

4 *Bear left then right for about 40 yards (37 m) along the road. Go left through the second gate beyond the roadside house. Follow a line of stiles diagonally right, down a series of fields.*

2 *Turn left at the top of the rise and join a farm track.*

1 *The walk starts from the B6270 opposite a solitary barn about ½ a mile (0.8 km) east of Feetham. Climb the steep tree-lined track. It is difficult to follow in its upper reaches but keep to the left of the stream without climbing any walls.*

Feetham Pasture

3 *Cross the moorland road and follow the direction of a signpost across rough pastureland to Blades. Look out for stiles to keep on course.*

5 *Turn left on a rough track and follow it downhill to the road. Turn right along the road.*

Ⓑ

Gallows Top

Ⓐ

Ⓒ

6 *Bear left at the road junction and go down to the bridge.*

Ⓓ

Feetham

Turnip House

Ⓔ

Low Row

Ⓖ

8 *At the signpost, go left away from the river and climb through trees to reach the road. Turn left to reach Feetham.*

Hatter's Roof Ⓕ

River Swale

7 *Cross the stile beside the ruined gate on the nearside of the bridge and turn left downstream, along the elevated river-bank.*

Isles Bridge

A Viewpoint. Swaledale and the heather-clad Grinton Moors.

B Gallows Top Farm; named after a gibbet which stood nearby.

C Viewpoint east towards a wooded section of the central dale.

D Blades. A typical Yorkshire Dales' hill settlement. Look for the date over the door of the last house on the right of the path.

E Each spring, purple orchids grow near the stream below Turnip House.

F The Swale drains a large area of moor to the north and west and can quickly reach alarming proportions, hence the need for such a high embankment.

G Viewpoint. Feetham stands on its sunny terrace well above the danger of flooding.

Walk 36
INGLEBOROUGH

8½ miles (13.7 km) Strenuous, not suitable in mist or bad weather; one climb of 1834 feet (559 m)

Over 150,000 people climb Ingleborough each year, most of them using the path from Ingleton, or from Chapel-le-Dale, if they are following the 'Three Peaks' route. As a result, parts of the mountain have become badly eroded and urgent, expensive remedial action has been necessary.

This walk climbs Ingleborough by a little-used footpath and is an attractive alternative to the more popular routes. If you would like to follow the nature trail on the final stages of the walk through Clapdale Woods, try to get hold of the descriptive leaflet beforehand, either from the National Park Information Centre near the car park in Clapham, or from the toll cottage at the entrance to Clapdale.

To the left of the Ingleton road and filling the valley bottom, the land is built on slates and coal-bearing shales, the original bed of an ancient tropical sea. Above Newby Cote Farm, limestone makes itself apparent by outcrops. This is topped by a moor, where shake holes and pot holes drain the surface water into underground caverns. Sandstone and shales take over around the 1500 foot (457 m) contour on Little Ingleborough. A final cap of gritstone guards the summit plateau of Ingleborough itself.

A Clapham. A charming village which grew around the Leeds–Kendal turnpike road, now superseded by the A65. There is a National Park Information Centre near the car park and several sources of refreshment.

B Viewpoint. Below, you can see the wide valley of the River Wenning, a tributary of the Lune, which flows into Morecambe Bay beyond Lancaster.

C Shake holes and pot holes are the surface indication of the hollow nature of limestone country. A shake hole is usually a depression in the surrounding moor but potholes are definite holes which often lead to subterranean caverns.

D Ingleborough. There is an often-missed panorama plate on top of the central column of the summit shelter. Other features include a pile of masonry above the escarpment to the west – the remains of a hospice tower built in 1830, which was destroyed not long after its erection. More interesting are the remains of a wall, said to be Roman, around the perimeter of the summit plateau and the clearly defined outlines of hut circles. Local folklore suggests that a British tribe held out here against Roman invaders before being tricked into surrender by one of their members. If the wall is Roman, it is likely that they used Ingleborough summit as a signal station: the mountain can be seen from a considerable distance in most directions.

E Gaping Gill. The best known British pothole; it falls in one single plunge of 340 feet (104 m) from the slippery, unprotected surface rocks. Water from Fell Beck falling into its depths drains eventually into a system which next sees daylight near the entrance to Ingleborough Cave. A winch is rigged each Spring Bank Holiday to lower visitors, as well as serious cavers, to the bottom of Gaping Gill.

F Ingleborough Cave. A show cave since 1837, the entrance is from the side of the path along Clapdale. Even though the stream issuing from its mouth has come from Gaping Gill, so far no caver has managed to penetrate the last few hundred yards which link the two.

G The delightful woodlands and limestone grotto are part of the grounds of Ingleborough Hall. Reginald Farrer (1880–1920), the international botanist and alpine flower specialist, lived here and planted clumps of bamboo and the Himalayan rhododendrons which bloom each spring in the woods. There is also a nature trail.

over

56

5 *Return by the same route, away from the summit, through a gap which was once the gateway of the Roman wall.*

6 *Go down the wide moorland path to Little Ingleborough. Then bear left from its summit, still downhill.*

4 *Turn left at the junction with a well-defined path. Cross Little Ingleborough and follow the broad ridge upwards to the giant steps leading to the main summit.*

7 *Follow the path, to the right, off the moor and into narrow Trow Gill.*

3 *The path is often indistinct. Keeping to the right of a line of shooting butts, climb directly up the hillside away from the corner of the wall. Continue in this direction when the shooting butts end. Aim for the summit of Little Ingleborough when it comes into view, above the limestone scars.*

8 *Follow the woodland path down Clapdale. A small toll is charged at the far end for the upkeep of these private woodlands. Clapdale woodlands are occasionally closed for pheasant shooting (Nov/Dec). If this should be the case, use the bridleway on the right and climb up to Clapdale Farm. Follow the farm access lane, to the left and down to Clapham village. There is no toll charge along this right of way.*

2 *Turn right along the farm drive but keep to the left of the main farm buildings. Follow the moorland track uphill and to the right of the boundary wall. Ignore any side tracks.*

9 *Pay the small toll at the cottage and then go to the left into the village.*

1 *Follow the old Ingleton road from Clapham for about 1½ miles (2.4 km) to Newby Cote. If you can arrange for transport, it will save road-walking along this section.*

Cairn

Cairns

Ingleborough

Little Ingleborough

Ingleborough Common

Swallow Hole

Area of Shake Holes

Gaping Gill

Trow Gill

Ingleborough Cave

Newby Cote

Clapdale Wood

Clapdale Drive

The Lake

Clapham

D C B E F G A

Walk 37
GARGRAVE
7½ miles (12 km) Easy, muddy sections after rain

Gargrave is just outside the southern boundary of the York-shire Dales National Park and also marks the boundary between the Yorkshire Dales and Craven, a district of lush pastures on land made from the debris left by a retreating ice sheet. As a one-time coaching village, Gargrave's links with these bygone traditions are maintained by a number of hospitable roadside inns which remind travellers on the modern A65 of more leisurely modes of transport.

Strategically placed in a central position within the Aire–Calder Gap, which is the widest low-level gap in the Pennines and a route used since prehistoric times, Gargrave has road, canal and rail links within its bound-aries. The Romans built a trans-Pennine road to the south of the town and, in more settled times, a prosperous local Roman family built their villa nearby. The A65 still follows the route of the Ken-dal to Keighley turnpike, which was opened in 1753 in order to bring Westmorland wool more easily to the mills of the West Riding. In 1770, an Act of Parlia-ment authorised the building of a canal to link Leeds to the Atlantic seaport of Liverpool but it took over 20 years to complete this difficult piece of water naviga-tion. The men who navigated or built the canals became known as 'navvies', a title which is still used to describe anyone who is en-gaged in heavy manual building work. The Leeds–Liverpool canal is the oldest of the three trans-Pennine canals and the only one still navigable. It is now used by holiday boats. With the coming of the railway era, canals began to lose their commercial traffic. The Leeds to Carlisle railway was opened in 1876; the line from Gargrave runs north to Settle and the start of the scenic Settle to Carlisle line.

Travellers of a uniquely mod-ern variety pass through Gargrave today in a steady stream along the Pennine Way. Here it follows one of its lowest and more rural sec-tions, a link between the heather moors above Earby and the limestone wonders of Malham Cove.

On this walk, the canal is fol-lowed all the way from Gargrave as far as East Marton, where the Pennine Way is joined. Lush green fields lining a series of low hummocky. hills are crossed by the well-marked path used by the Pennine Way on its journey from East Marton to Gargrave.

A Old wharfs and canal-side buildings have been adapted for modern use as grain warehouses and offices. Today, mostly plea-sure craft use the canal but the very rare commercial boat still plys its leisurely way through a section of the countryside which has remained unchanged for over 200 years.

B Locks enable canal traffic to climb up and down hills. Wider sections of the canal serve the dual purpose of storing water needed to supply the locks and of providing 'winding holes' or turning places for the boats.

C Early canal builders preferred to use the contours of the land, thereby reducing the need for a large number of locks, which are expensive to build and maintain and also require a great deal of water to work them.

D The walk follows the well-signposted Pennine Way route from East Marton all the way to Gargrave.

E Viewpoint. Gargrave and the wild limestone moors of Upper Airedale can be glimpsed from Scaleber Hill. The green hum-mocky landscape is made from boulder clay deposited by retreat-ing glaciers and melt waters after they had breached the Aire Gap during the last Ice Age. The rolling nature of the countryside is unsuitable for extensive ploughing but makes excellent grazing for dairy cattle.

over

0   1 mile

0   1 km

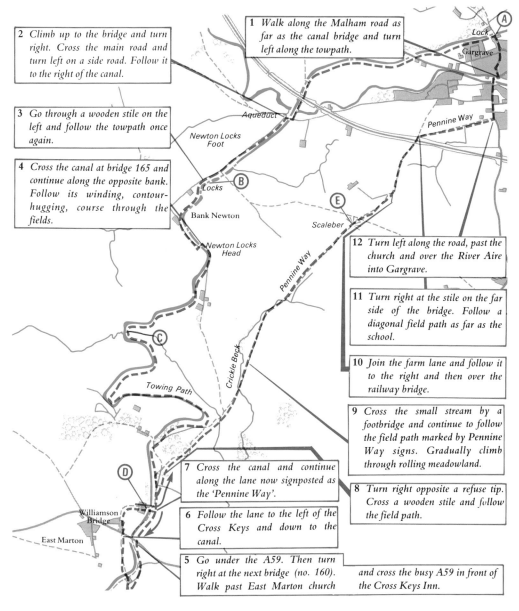

1 *Walk along the Malham road as far as the canal bridge and turn left along the towpath.*

2 *Climb up to the bridge and turn right. Cross the main road and turn left on a side road. Follow it to the right of the canal.*

3 *Go through a wooden stile on the left and follow the towpath once again.*

4 *Cross the canal at bridge 165 and continue along the opposite bank. Follow its winding, contour-hugging, course through the fields.*

12 *Turn left along the road, past the church and over the River Aire into Gargrave.*

11 *Turn right at the stile on the far side of the bridge. Follow a diagonal field path as far as the school.*

10 *Join the farm lane and follow it to the right and then over the railway bridge.*

9 *Cross the small stream by a footbridge and continue to follow the field path marked by Pennine Way signs. Gradually climb through rolling meadowland.*

8 *Turn right opposite a refuse tip. Cross a wooden stile and follow the field path.*

7 *Cross the canal and continue along the lane now signposted as the 'Pennine Way'.*

6 *Follow the lane to the left of the Cross Keys and down to the canal.*

5 *Go under the A59. Then turn right at the next bridge (no. 160). Walk past East Marton church and cross the busy A59 in front of the Cross Keys Inn.*

59

INGLETON'S WATERFALLS

4½ miles (7.2km) Moderate, slippery areas when wet; one climb of 500 feet (152m)

This is probably the most beautiful walk in the Yorkshire Dales. For most of the way, the footpath is privately owned and, as a result, a small admission fee is charged, but this will be of little consequence when balanced against the privilege of walking in such delightful surroundings.

Two rivers, the Doe and Twiss, join below Ingleton to become the Greta, itself a tributary of the Lune, one of the two Dales' rivers flowing into Morecambe Bay (the other is the Ribble). Upstream from Ingleton, the Doe and Twiss, after their birth on the opposite side of Whernside, flow through flat-bottomed upper valleys before cascading down tree-lined limestone gorges. The walk follows their course in a clockwise direction, upstream along the Twiss, then down the Doe.

Much of the geology of the Ingleton area is revealed by the rivers' flow. Around the car park, the underlying rock is mostly shale and slate, which accounts for the comparatively flat land to the west. Harder slates form the river-bed upstream for most of the way and the more easily eroded limestones have been worn into glens and gorges where natural amphitheatres are slowly being cut back under the force of their waterfalls. Above the narrowest of these gorges, further slate deposits resist the downward action of the rivers, making their course more gentle. In the higher parts of the upper dale, where the main limestone beds are found, any water soon disappears underground, not emerging until it meets the impervious lower slate beds.

Spring is the best time to appreciate the walk, when the water levels of both rivers are still fairly high and the delicate green of newly leafed trees form a backcloth but don't screen the views of the deeper ravines.

Parking and refreshments are available at the beginning of the walk. Approach the car park by driving through Ingleton from either the A65 Settle road or the B6255 Hawes road and then follow the side road steeply down into the valley. Access to the car park is well signposted from the village.

A The outward section of the walk follows the River Twiss upstream. Its waterfalls tend to be wider than the Doe's and are best seen face on. Those of the Doe are mostly in tree-lined narrow ravines, which are more dramatic when viewed from above. Both rivers join a few yards below the road which leads into the car park.

B Pecca Falls, a series of narrow cascades. There is usually a hut open on the nearby hillside, where refreshments are on sale.

C Thornton Force. The highest waterfall — 46 feet (14m) — in the Ingleton area and, scenically, the most attractive. The tree-fringed limestone crag makes a natural amphitheatre. The darker rock beneath the falls is slate which, unlike limestone, is impervious to water.

D Beezley Falls. The first cascade of the hitherto peaceful River Doe. The river's other name is the Greta, a title which is retained by the main river below Ingleton. Outcrops and boulders in the river-bed cause the stream to make several dramatic changes of its direction.

E Snow Falls. One of a series of three in the section of the valley known as Twistleton Glen.

F The quarry, here, once exploited the harder but more easily worked slate which forms the bed-rock of this normally limestone region.

G Cat Leap Fall. A little off route, on the left, this fall is the final exuberant act of Skirwith Beck, a side stream which joins the Doe close by an old limestone quarry.

over

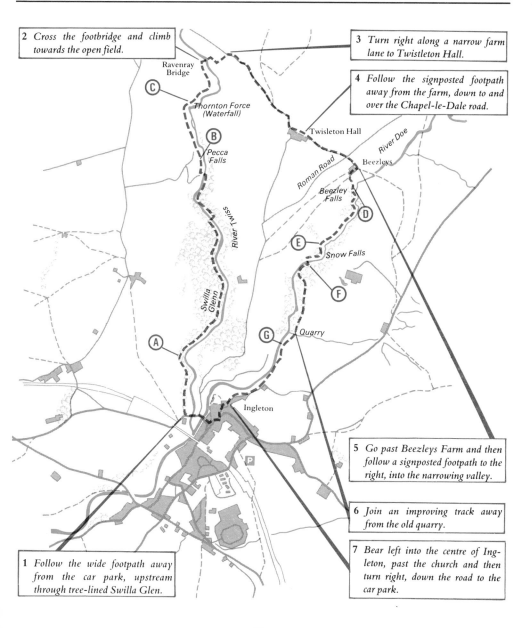

2 *Cross the footbridge and climb towards the open field.*

3 *Turn right along a narrow farm lane to Twistleton Hall.*

4 *Follow the signposted footpath away from the farm, down to and over the Chapel-le-Dale road.*

Ravenray Bridge

Ⓒ

Thornton Force (Waterfall)

Twisleton Hall

River Doe

Ⓑ

Pecca Falls

Roman Road

Beezleys

Beezley Falls

Ⓓ

River Twiss

Ⓔ

Snow Falls

Swilla Glenn

Ⓕ

Ⓐ

Ⓖ *Quarry*

Ingleton

Ⓟ

5 *Go past Beezleys Farm and then follow a signposted footpath to the right, into the narrowing valley.*

6 *Join an improving track away from the old quarry.*

7 *Bear left into the centre of Ingleton, past the church and then turn right, down the road to the car park.*

1 *Follow the wide footpath away from the car park, upstream through tree-lined Swilla Glen.*

CAM END AND LING GILL
6¼ miles (10 km) Moderate/strenuous; one climb of 390 feet (119 m)

Here is a walk to link short stretches of the Dales Way and the Pennine Way. The section which follows the Dales Way from Gearstones uses part of the Roman road from Lancaster to Bainbridge. It joins the Pennine Way at Cam End – a green road used originally as a drove road but now used by Pennine Wayfar-

ers. For the return to Gearstones, this track will lead you down past Ling Gill to Old Ing Farm where farm tracks and footpaths cross the moors.

Parking is limited around the farm settlement of Gearstones. Be careful not to block access to farm entrances or field gates. The large building in the middle of

the group was once an inn, used by Scottish drovers moving the half wild black Galloway cattle to southern markets. The house stands at the side of the B6255 Ribblehead to Hawes road about 1½ miles (2.4 km) north-east of the viaduct.

A Gearstones Lodge. A building has stood on the site for centuries. It was once an inn giving accommodation to cattle drovers who passed this way south along Cam High Road. The track was linked in its turn to other roads and trackways to the north and south; some are now metalled roads but others have almost disappeared.

B A signpost will indicate that the track is part of the Dales Way. Its foundations are Roman, although nothing remains of the original road other than the route.

C Low circular stone and turf walls on the left of the track could be mistaken for prehistoric relics but they are, in fact, modern shooting butts. Red grouse, the target of sportsmen in late summer and autumn, give themselves away by their low, erratic flight patterns and cries of 'ge-beck, ge-beck'.

D The track is now part of the Horton to Hawes section of the Pennine Way.

E Viewpoint. The Three Peaks can be seen from this point. From left to right are Penyghent, Ingleborough and Whernside, the latter two towering above Ribblehead viaduct. The circuit of these steep mountains is a hard day's expedition for most walkers but fell runners manage to complete the race in a few hours.

F Ling Gill Bridge. A plaque set into the upstream parapet of the bridge tells us that in 1765 it was repaired at 'the charge of the whole West Rideing (sic)', an indication of its once greater importance.

G Ling Gill National Nature Reserve. The limestone gorge on the right is filled with woodland, the remnant of forests which once covered much of the limestone dales. It is possible to enter Ling Gill to examine the plants at close quarters but on no account

may any be taken without a permit from the Regional Controller. Most of the gill can be seen from the track but if you go into the reserve, take great care on the slippery edge of the ravine.

H Calf Holes. A pothole is over the wall on the left, at the start of the double walled section of the track. Water cascading into its depths reappears about ½ a mile (0.8 km) away to the north-west at Browgill Cave.

I God's Bridge. A wide natural arch formed by Blow Gill Beck tunnelling through a weakness in the limestone surface rocks.

J Viewpoint. The deep-cut little valley to the south-west is Thorns Gill, an unspoilt natural habitat for wild flowers in its wooded lower reaches, ½ a mile (0.8 km) downstream. Ingleborough, Ribblehead Viaduct and Whernside can be glimpsed from the slopes leading down to the footbridge.

over

Walk 39
Cam End and Ling Gill
continued

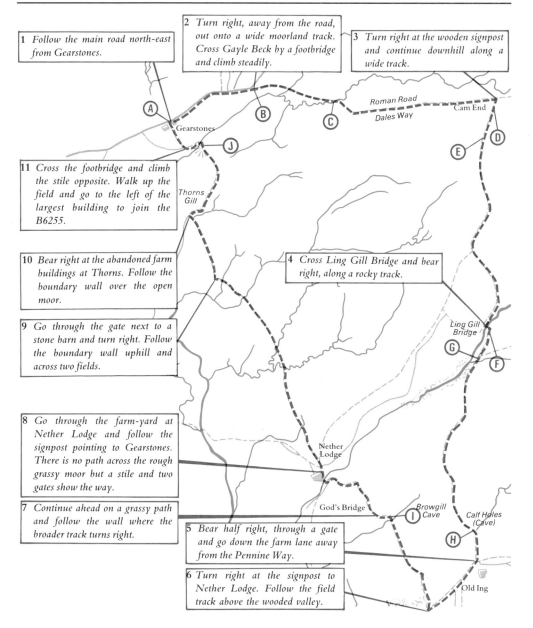

1 Follow the main road north-east from Gearstones.

2 Turn right, away from the road, out onto a wide moorland track. Cross Gayle Beck by a footbridge and climb steadily.

3 Turn right at the wooden signpost and continue downhill along a wide track.

11 Cross the footbridge and climb the stile opposite. Walk up the field and go to the left of the largest building to join the B6255.

10 Bear right at the abandoned farm buildings at Thorns. Follow the boundary wall over the open moor.

4 Cross Ling Gill Bridge and bear right, along a rocky track.

9 Go through the gate next to a stone barn and turn right. Follow the boundary wall uphill and across two fields.

8 Go through the farm-yard at Nether Lodge and follow the signpost pointing to Gearstones. There is no path across the rough grassy moor but a stile and two gates show the way.

7 Continue ahead on a grassy path and follow the wall where the broader track turns right.

5 Bear half right, through a gate and go down the farm lane away from the Pennine Way.

6 Turn right at the signpost to Nether Lodge. Follow the field track above the wooded valley.

Gearstones

Roman Road
Dales Way
Cam End

Thorns Gill

Ling Gill Bridge

Nether Lodge

God's Bridge

Browgill Cave

Calf Holes (Cave)

Old Ing

A B C D E F G H I J

63

Walk 40
CHAPEL-LE-DALE
3½ miles (5.6 km) Easy

The walk starts near the chapel which gives the hamlet of Chapel-le-Dale its name. Access is by the side road which leaves the B6255 below the Hill Inn and is about 3½ miles (5.6km) north-east of Ingleton.

As the route is entirely along farm lanes, it is suitable in all weathers.

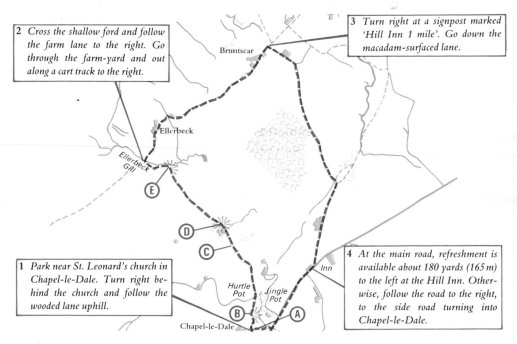

2 Cross the shallow ford and follow the farm lane to the right. Go through the farm-yard and out along a cart track to the right.

3 Turn right at a signpost marked 'Hill Inn 1 mile'. Go down the macadam-surfaced lane.

Bruntscar

Ellerbeck

Ellerbeck Gill

E

D

C

Inn

Hurtle Pot

Jingle Pot

B

A

Chapel-le-Dale

1 Park near St. Leonard's church in Chapel-le-Dale. Turn right behind the church and follow the wooded lane uphill.

4 At the main road, refreshment is available about 180 yards (165 m) to the left at the Hill Inn. Otherwise, follow the road to the right, to the side road turning into Chapel-le-Dale.

A St. Leonard's church. Inside this simple Dales church is a memorial to the men who died, either from injury or cholera while building Ribblehead Viaduct and the Settle to Dent section of the Leeds to Carlisle railway.

B Viewpoint. The massive bulk of Ingleborough towers above tree-shrouded Hurtle Pot, which is reputed to be the home of a boggard. A boggard is a Dales' sprite, who can be friendly or mischievous depending on how he is treated.

C Sculpture piece. A plaque on the unexpected piece of sculpture at the side of the lane tells its story.

D Viewpoint. Gill Head House makes a pleasant foreground to the backward view of Inglebor-ough. Turn around and the long whale-back ridge of Whernside fills the skyline. Ingleborough is composed mostly of limestone but Whernside's rocks are mainly shales and gritstones above a base of limestone which fills the dale on all sides of Chapel-le-Dale.

E Ribblehead Viaduct. This dramatic man-made feature spanning the dale head fits well within the moorland landscape.